Making the Most of Your

SEWING MACHINE
&
SERGER
ACCESSORIES

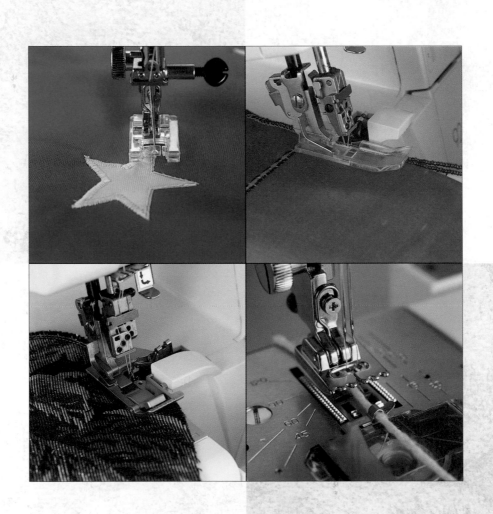

Making the Most of Your

SEWING MACHINE
&
SERGER
ACCESSORIES

JoAnn Pugh-Gannon

Sterling Publishing Co., Inc.
New York

A Sterling/Sewing Information Resources Book

Sewing Information Resources

Owner: JoAnn Pugh-Gannon
Photography: Kaz Ayukawa, K Graphics
Book Design and Electronic Page Layout: Ernie Shelton, Shelton Design Studios
Index: Mary Helen Schiltz

Sewing Information Resources is a registered trademark of GANZ Inc.

Library of Congress Cataloging-in-Publication Data Available.

Pugh-Gannon, JoAnn.
    Making the most of your sewing machine & serger accessories / JoAnn Pugh-Gannon.
        p.   cm.
    "A Sterling/sewing information resources book."
    Includes index.
    ISBN 0-8069-8453-8
    1. Machine sewing. 2. Serging. I. Title.
TT713. P82   1999
646.2--dc21   98-50985
                                                                CIP

A Sterling/Sewing Information Resources Book

10   9   8   7   6   5   4   3   2   1

First paperback edition published in 2000 by
Sterling Publishing Company, Inc.
387 Park Avenue South, New York, N.Y. 10016
© 1999 by JoAnn Pugh-Gannon
Distributed in Canada by Sterling Publishing
% Canadian Manda Group, One Atlantic Avenue, Suite 105
Toronto, Ontario, Canada M6K 3E7
Distributed in Great Britain and Europe by Cassell PLC
Wellington House, 125 Strand, London WC2R 0BB, England
Distributed in Australia by Capricorn Link (Australia) Pty Ltd.
P.O. Box 6651, Baulkham Hills, Business Centre, NSW 2153, Australia
Printed in China
All rights reserved

Sterling ISBN 0-8069-8453-8 Trade
            0-8069-8205-5 Paper

ABOUT THE AUTHOR

JoAnn Pugh-Gannon has been involved within the home sewing industry for many years. Her first position as an educational representative with Simplicity Pattern Company led to a long career with Swiss Bernina, later known as Bernina of America, the United States importer of Swiss-made Bernina sewing machines and related products. As Vice-President of Marketing Software for Bernina, she was responsible for all dealer and consumer education, educational materials, and Bernina University. In 1994, she began publishing sewing and craft books under the name of Sewing Information Resources.

ACKNOWLEDGEMENTS

A very special thank you to Chris Tryon at Elna USA for all her timely assistance in getting this book completed. Also to Elna USA for their generous supply of machines and accessories for use in samplemaking and photography.

Sample making by: Karen Kunkel, Chris James, Sara Hochhauser, and JoAnn Pugh-Gannon

CONTENTS

GETTING STARTED 8

THREADS, NEEDLES, FABRICS, AND NOTIONS 10

YOUR SEWING MACHINE AND SERGER ACCESSORIES 15

PROJECTS: LET'S DECORATE 30

SIMPLE CHAIR COVER 32

SERGER MEMORY BOXES 34

PEARLY BATHROOM 36

SWEET DREAMS PILLOWS 38

RECYCLED SWEATERS 42

CLASSY COVERS 44

TASSELED RUNNER 46

TIERED TABLECLOTHS 48

BELTLOOP PILLOWS 50

STARS GALORE 54

ELEGANT NECKROLL 56

TRIMMED CHERRY VALANCE 58

PERFECT PICNIC TRIMMINGS 60

KID'S ORGANIZER 64

PROJECTS: LET'S DRESS UP 66

EASY APPLIQUÉD DRESS 68

CLASSIC BAGS 70

PEARL-EDGED SHAWL 74

REVERSIBLE APRONS 76

SILKY BLOUSE AND COLLAR 78

HATS AND ROSES 82

BLANKET-STITCH VEST 84

FAGOTED SKIRT AND TOP 87

HEIRLOOM HANKIE 90

BATH WRAP, MITT & SLIPPERS 92

MAKE-UP ROLL 95

TRIMMED KNIT PJ'S 98

VEST O' TECHNIQUES 100

UPHOLSTERY JACKET 103

CLASSIC SPORT TOTE 106

SILK EVENING BAGS 108

STAMPED FAUX VEST 111

A JACKET OF TRICKS 114

APPENDIX: MAKING BIAS STRIPS 119

NECESSARY PATTERNS 120

METRIC CHARTS 125

INDEX 126

GETTING STARTED

Becoming familiar with your sewing or overlock machine and all its accessories can be a fun and exciting process. Depending on the make and model of machine you own, it offers endless stitch possibilities and opportunities for you to be creative in your sewing and serging. Whether the stitches are built-in, cassettes are added, or you develop them yourself with machine length and width manipulation or tension adjustments, the fun is just about to begin.

And don't forget the many accessories that can be used on your machines. Try just one or try them all. Both the sewing machine and the serger offer many unique and different accessories to be creative with. It may take a little practice, sometimes more patience, but the results can be well worth your time and effort. Don't be afraid to experiment. The more you know about your accessories, the easier your sewing and serging will be. It will become second nature to pick up a gathering foot rather than use a long stitch for soft ruffles, make and attach piping in one step rather than two, or attach binding quickly and easily.

Try new threads and fabrics on both machines. And remember, your serger doesn't have to be used only on knit fabrics. Edging stitches executed with beautiful heavy rayon threads on wools, fleece, or home decorating fabrics can't be duplicated. Rolled hems stitched with woolly nylon thread can be the perfect edge finish with the serger for napkins, scarves, or collars and cuffs. Hem a skirt or insert a zipper. The choices are unlimited and easily accomplished using your many accessories.

So forge ahead and use the projects in this book as a jumping off point. Use them to practice your techniques, expand your imagination, become comfortable with the many accessories, or just make some fun things. Many of the projects included here, involve both the sewing machine and serger. Learn to use both machines comfortably. Certainly you can make a garment or craft item completely on either machine but it's more fun to discover the strengths of both and learn how perfectly they compliment each other.

THREADS, NEEDLES, FABRICS, AND NOTIONS

Part of the fun in beginning any sewing or serging project is just in the choosing of your fabrics, threads, and notions. Mixing and matching colors, fabric types, textures and weights, or adding twists and turns to a favorite pattern makes the process exciting and creative. Be innovative in your thinking. Experiment with new threads or fabrics. Play with your machines! Just because the instruction manual says "this stitch is used for...", don't be afraid to stretch the boundaries and try something new. Just have fun!

THREADS

Let's first explore all of the thread possibilities there are for you to choose from. Rayon, cotton, metallic, yarn, woolly nylon, monofilament, polyester, and ribbon floss are just a few of the many decorative choices that may work on your sewing machine or serger. Select the appropriate thread for the look or effect you want to achieve on your project. Also check the care label on the spool. Match the thread care with the garment care you plan for your project.

Most machines are set-up or calibrated to a specific polyester thread for general sewing and serging. Check with your dealer about the thread that is matched to your machine. On your serger, you may experience slightly more tension adjustments on a variety of fabrics if not using the specific thread for your machine. Why? Thread has weight or thickness. This thickness obviously affects the tension controls.

Thread quality is also an important factor to consider when sewing and serging. As the saying goes, "You get what you pay for" is true in this case. Purchase quality thread for your

projects. A quality thread may still break when serging but that is not necessarily a factor of the thread but may be the stitch selection or a very high tension on the thread. As you will discover with your serger as with your sewing machine, the thread, needle(s), fabric, and even the tension needs to work together amicably!

On your sewing machine, some threads work better through the needle, some are wound on the bobbin and sewn from the reverse, or heavier threads are best couched on the top. Test both the thread and your stitch selection on sample fabric before starting your project. Many times a mistake may produce just the result you desire!

Most threads can be used successfully in the upper and lower loopers on

the serger as well as the needle(s). When selecting your stitch, choose the thread accordingly. For instance, if you want to stitch a decorative chain stitch, use the heavier thread in the chain looper. However, if you have selected a blanket stitch, the heavier thread is threaded through the needle.

Generally, thread wound on cones is designed for serger use, however, domestic-type spools can be used on both machines. There are a number of thread holders on the market today that will accommodate cone thread for use on the sewing machine. For the serger remember to use either cone holders or spool caps based on the type of thread put-up you are using.

A variety of threads have been used for the projects in this book including metallics, woolly nylon, Pearl Crown Rayon, rayon embroidery thread #40, and polyester sewing thread. As you work through the projects, you will become very comfortable with these threads and their characteristics. On your serger, fine tuning the tensions will become easier so you get the effect you want.

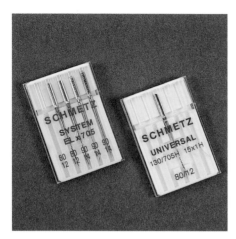

Needles are also an important part of your sewing and serging success. There are many different types of needles on the market today based on the thread being used or the type of project being sewn. Universal, sharp, machine embroidery, topstitching, metallica, or quilting are just a few of the many needles available. Select the needle carefully for each project. Check your machine manual for any particular adjustments necessary with specific needles. For instance, be sure to watch your stitch width when using double or triple needles on your sewing machine.

Selecting the correct type of needle for your serger is essential. Check your instruction manual for this information. Industrial and household needles are not interchangeable so be sure to check carefully for your brand of machine. Some manufacturers, such as Elna, may have a household system (EL x 705) specific to their machine. This needle system is recommended particularly when using the cover hem.

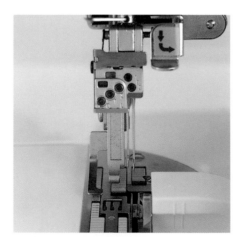

Sergers today have numerous needle positions available for the variety of stitch formations built into each machine. Usually labeled in some manner, be sure to use the correct position and needle combination for the stitch selected. When inserting the needles, always make sure they are in their highest position to avoid breakage or tension problems.

Needle size is determined by the thickness of the thread. Universal sewing needles are used for general sewing, but specialty needles may need to be used for unusual fabrics or threads. Topstitching needles with larger eyes are needed with threads such as Pearl Crown Rayon, while embroidery, quilting, stretch, metallica, or microtec needles might be needed on unique fabrics or with specific threads. Again, select the correct size and type of needle for each project. It may require some testing to find the perfect combination but your final results are important.

FABRICS

There are so many types of fabrics available to the sewer today that a discussion of fabrics could take an entire book! The manufacturing process, fabric content, and sewing techniques have changed dramatically over the years. The challenge of sewing is mixing the ingredients together and coming up with the perfect end result.

Don't be afraid to experiment. In general, sewers are creative people and the more fun you have with each project, the more projects you will sew! One of the objectives of this book is to encourage you to learn more about your sewing machine and serger. The extra accessories just open the door to more creativity. Don't miss the opportunity to wander down new sewing paths.

Your sewing machine can handle most any fabric type you put under the presser foot. Match the needle to the fabric by size and type. An extra-large needle may harm a beautiful silk and a fine needle won't penetrate an upholstery weight. Once again, choose the correct size and type needle with the thread for the fabric you are working with.

A common myth is that sergers are for sewing knit fabrics only. Your serger should be able to stitch over any number of fabric types. Silkies or cottons, decorator fabrics or fleece — your serger should be able to handle it all. Again depending on the stitch selection, some fabrics will require a little extra care and machine adjustment. A rolled hem on a wiry fabric, such as the linen used in the Heirloom Hankie, may require an increased upper looper tension, a decreased cutting width or a shorter stitch length. Spray starch also helped control this fabric. It is always best to test the stitch on the fabric prior to completing your project.

There are so many sewing notions on the market today that in some cases it is hard to choose your favorite. You will find some more valuable than others like with any hobby.

Most sewing machines come with basic supplies such as a lint brush, seam ripper, additional bobbins, and a hem gauge. Depending on the model of machine, some come with more or less supplies and presser feet.

Sergers come with a number of accessories either built-into the housing or contained in an accessory box or pouch. Tweezers are essential for threading everything from loopers to needles. Some manufacturers provide needle threaders but there are many types available through your dealer or notions catalogs. A single or double needle insertion tool helps with changing needles around for multiple needle stitches.

There are a number of supplies or notions that are essential for all types of sewing. Seam sealant is used to control thread ends from raveling, buttonholes from fraying, or keeping nylon stocking from running! After threading the ends back through the serger stitching with a bodkin, add seam sealant to fix the ends. When crossing corners with a machine or serger rolled hem, such as done on napkins or scarves, seal the corners with sealant.

Paper tape or masking tape controls the ends of opened thread spools. Basting tape or fabric glue hold zippers in place before stitching. A bodkin, a point turner, bias tape makers, a mat and rotary cutter are just some of the supplies every sewing room should contain. And don't forget a good pair of scissors. Check the notions board at your local fabric store or let your fingers do the walking through sewing notions catalogs. You will certainly find the sewing tools and notions you can't live without!

YOUR SEWING MACHINE AND SERGING ACCESSORIES

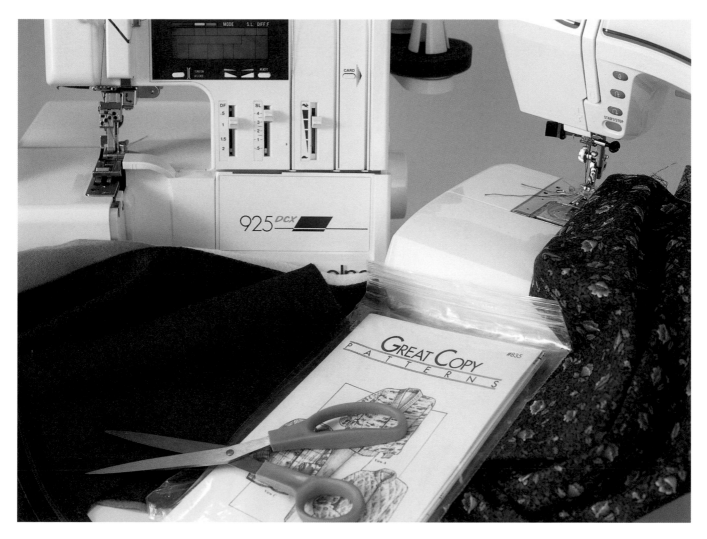

Every sewing machine and serger comes with a variety of presser feet based on the capabilities of the machine. However, there are any number of additional accessories available for all makes and models. Check with your local sewing machine dealer to find out what additional feet are available for your machine. The more you know how to use your presser feet the more fun you will have sewing and the more efficient you will be. Listed below are just some of the accessories you may find helpful in making your sewing projects easier.

Known by many names, satin stitch foot, appliqué foot, or embroidery foot, these feet all do the same thing — provide smooth stitching for a compressed zig zag stitch. The underside of the foot is grooved in such a manner so it will ride over the satin stitching easily. Some manufacturers have more than one foot with these names. Be sure to check the size of the groove on the bottom as the width of the zig zag should be able to ride smoothly under the foot. These feet are plastic or metal and some have the center section removed for better visibility but all perform the same function.

The standard presser foot with most sewing machines accommodates both zig zag and straight stitching. It may be metal or plastic in composition. The plastic foot may provide better visibility in certain situations whereas the metal foot provides stability in some cases.

While a straight stitch can be sewn with the standard foot, certain fabrics may require the use of a straight stitch foot. Stitching on fine, sheer, or silky fabrics may be easier with this presser foot as it holds the fabric more firmly around the needle hole.

The blindhem foot is an essential foot and is usually standard with most machines. Designed to assist in easy hemming, this foot has a bar that rides against the roll of the fabric for straight guiding. This foot also becomes indispensable for edgestitching, topstitching, or any kind of straight stitching necessary. Move the needle position to the setting desired for your project and use the foot as a guide and just sew!

Most machines have an overlock or overcasting foot. These feet usually have a pin along one side to prevent single knit fabrics from rolling up while stitching. The swing of the needle clears the pin during stitch formation keeping the fabric flat.

The zipper foot is a standard accessory with all machines. Needle positions are changed or the foot is snaped onto the shank on a different side to position the stitching in the correct place on the edge of the zipper tapes.

A button-sewing foot is a foot that is so simple to use you'll never sew on another button by hand! This foot anchors the button while the zig zag stitch secures the button in place.

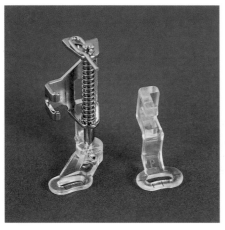

With the advent of embroidery machines to the market, most machines, top-of-the-line at least, now come with a darning foot. Originally used for free-hand darning or embroidery, these feet now have a new life with the many exciting embroidery capabilities of the computerized machines. Check your sewing machine manual for the correct foot for your darning or embroidery project.

Piecing is easier with a patchwork or 1/4" foot. This foot helps ensure a perfect 1/4" seam allowance on any quilting project. Usually a straight stitch foot, this foot may have markings on the toes for matching corners.

The multi-cord foot is the ideal foot for couching one or more threads on your project. The heavy decorative threads slide under the black guide and are held in place while stitching.

Gathering long lengths of fabric is accomplished with the gathering foot. Increased tension and a long stitch length helps the foot gather the fabric quickly and easily.

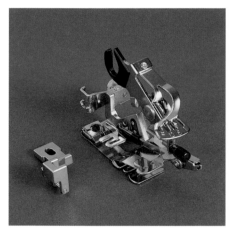

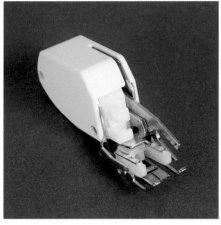

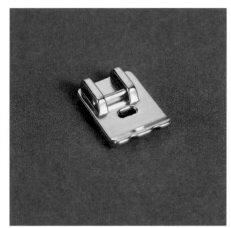

A ruffler is another attachment used to gather or ruffle fabric. A larger attachment than a gathering foot, the ruffler will ruffle and pleat single and double layers of fabric and attach gathered trims to a flat layer.

Another indispensable accessory is the walking, even-feed, or looping sole foot. The upper feed dogs work with the machine feed dogs to keep the fabric layers together. Perfect for matching plaids, stitching silky fabrics, or quilting many layers, a walking foot is hard to live without.

Making and attaching piping becomes easier with a pearl and piping foot. Wrap the cord with bias, adjust the needle position, and stitch. When attaching the cord, move the needle position one step over and stitch again.

Piping and mini-piping can also be sewn with the beading foot. The groove is centered under the foot and corresponds to the size of the cording. Cords and beads also can be couched with a simple zig zag stitch.

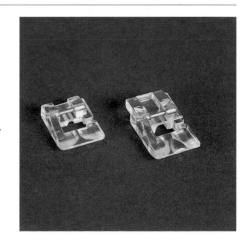

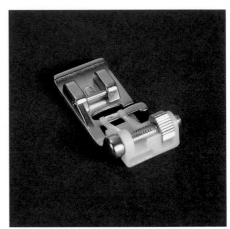

Hemming feet are very useful feet for finishing edges. Each hemming foot is sized for the weight of the fabric being rolled. The groove on the bottom holds the roll in place while stitching takes place.

Pintucks, corded or uncorded, are a delicate embellishment and simple to stitch using a tucking foot and guide. The cord is guided under the foot and rows of tiny tucks can be sewn right next to each other. The weight of the fabric and size of cord determines the tucking foot to use. Select the correct double needle for each foot.

Sequins and narrow ribbons are couched using the sequin and ribbon foot. An adjustable guide on the front keeps the trims straight and in place while stitching.

Stitch bias binding easily to the edges of your projects using the bias binder attachment. Single or double fold bias tape will feed evenly through this foot.

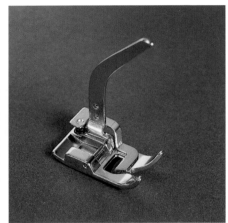

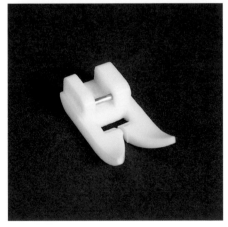

Fagoting is a decorative technique used to join two fabrics together with the fagoting foot and guide. A heavier thread is used on the bobbin and the guide keeps the fabrics a distance apart. Any number of decorative stitches may be used to bridge between two fabrics.

Fine tricot fabric is handled during stitching with the tricot foot. This foot keeps the fabric flat and eliminates pulling into the needle hole on the needle plate.

Stitch on vinyl, suede, plastics, or fabrics that may stick to the bottom of the presser foot with a roller or Teflon™ foot. The gnarled roller on the front of the roller foot and the Teflon sole helps feed the fabric smoothly under the foot.

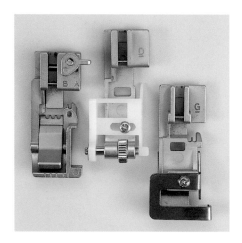

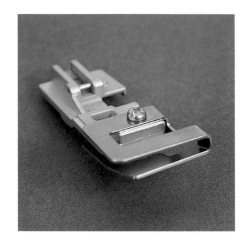

Your overlock machine is fitted with a standard presser foot that is capable of producing a variety of stitches both basic and utilitarian. Whether you own a 2-, 3-, 4-, or 5-thread machine, this foot provides the stitcher with any number of combinations. The stretch knit, 2- or 3-thread flatlock, 2- or 3-thread rolled hem, and stretched wrapped are just some of the stitches utilizing the standard presser foot.

Many standard presser feet are drilled with a small hole for feeding cords, fishline, or decorative threads to couch or use for other purposes. Serge with a rolled hem stitch over a filler cord to create your own braids and trims. The foot is versatile so be sure to explore all of it's possibilities.

Gathering a single or double thickness of fabric or gathering one fabric to a flat piece can be accomplished using the serger gathering foot. Depending on the weight of the fabric, your piece will be gathered more or less. Increase the stitch length or needle tension, adjust the foot pressure or the differential feed or pull the needle thread by hand to gather more.

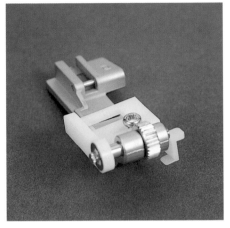

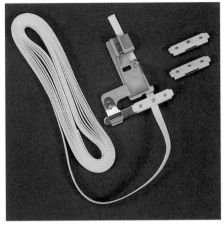

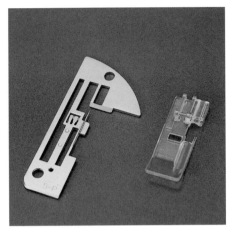

The blindhem foot is a versatile foot. Used to stitch a commercial-looking blindhem, this adjustable foot makes hemming easy. The hem is enclosed with the serger stitch while trimming any excess fabric at the same time.

A multi-purpose foot is also multi-functional. Designed to hold elastic, the foot guides flat elastic with little difficulty. The adjusting screw controls the amount of gathering. Holes on the stabilizer bar also can be used to feed cords for couching.

The pearl foot and needle plate guides strands of pearls or beads easily because of the deep groove on the bottom of the foot. Attached with a flatlock stitch, the pearls can accent the edge or middle of your project.

A bias binder attachment is also available for your serger. This accessory double folds a flat piece of bias tape to a width of approximately 3/8" and is attached with a chain stitch.

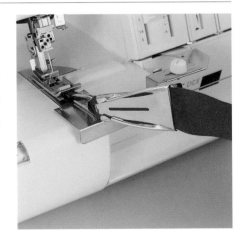

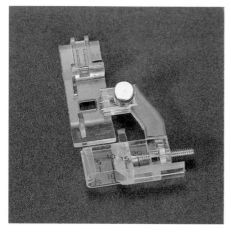
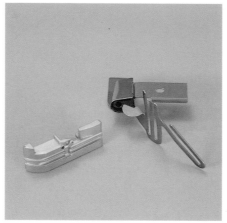
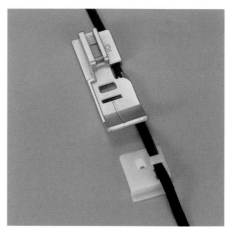

Some machines accommodate an accessory called the adjustable bias binder. This foot accommodates either purchased pre-folded or self-made bias tape of different widths resulting in a finished binding up to 1 inch. Use either the chain stitch or cover hem stitch to attach the bias tape.

Make and insert piping into a seam with the piping foot and tape guide. Designed for lightweight cottons, the tape guide controls and guides the cord and bias tape at the same time. Piping can also be stitched separately as the groove under the foot guides the cord.

The tape foot and tape and cord guide is perfect for all types of projects. Couch narrow ribbon, create your own decorative trims, or add bands of soutache to your next garment. The guide handles the narrow trim without worry.

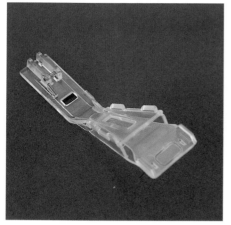

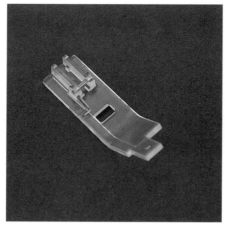

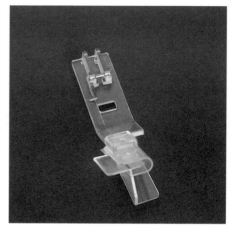

The beltloop foot is a very versatile foot. It not only can be used for practical purposes — making belt loops — but it also can be used in many decorative ways.

The cover hem foot is the standard foot used with a number of cover hem snap-on attachments. Being a clear foot it allows the stitcher a full view of the fabric and stitching.

Snap on a lace attachment guide and add flat or gathered lace or trims to the underside of a turned hem with the cover hem stitch. The edge is stitched before the side seams are sewn for best results.

A 1" hem guide, makes hemming with the cover hem stitch very easy. Press under a 1" hem and finish cuffs, pant or shirt hems quickly. This attachment works best on flat pieces and can be utilized with the cover hem, cover hem wide, or triple cover hem stitches.

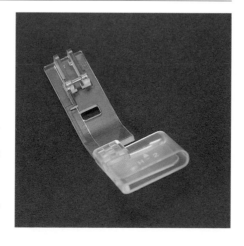

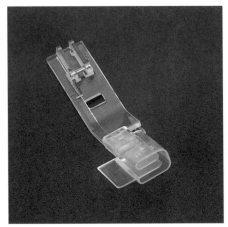 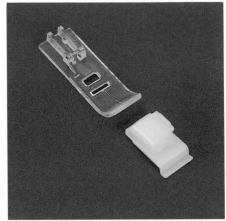 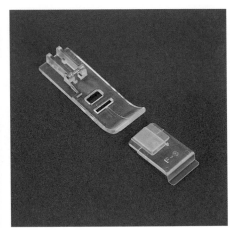

Using pre-folded bias tape, a wrapped seam guide helps you finish the raw edges at necklines or armholes, trim cuffs or add a decorative detail to any garment or accessory. Use the loopy cover hem side, right side out, to duplicate ready-to-wear details.

Other cover hem accessories attach to the machine in front of the foot rather than to the foot directly. One of those accessories, a felling guide makes serging flat felled seams an easy job. The guide controls the fabric while you are serging with the cover hem stitch.

A second option for attaching lace or trims to any project is with a lacing guide. The lace or trim is serged on top of the fabric edge with the cover hem stitch.

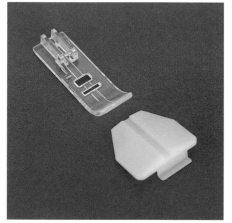

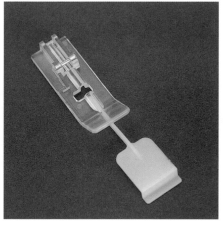

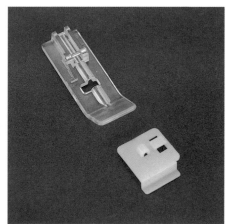

Topstitching details can be added by using a topstitch covered seam foot and guide. The guide attaches to the machine in front of the foot. The sewn seam follows in the groove of the guide and the straight stitching of the cover hem falls on each side of the sewn seam.

The pintuck foot and guide comes in two versions. One foot and guide is used for uncorded pintucks or tiny tucks. The guide lifts the fabric into the tuck while stitching.

A different guide is used for corded pintucks. The cording is threaded through the tape guide and then stitched into the pintuck. This is the same guide used with the taping foot for stitching down flat narrow tapes or trims with a flatlock stitch.

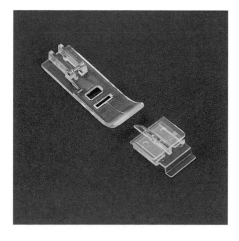

The fagoting guide assists in guiding two separate fabric edges under the foot while the cover hem stitch creates a lacy fagoting in between. Join like fabrics, attach lace to fabric, lace to lace, or try any number of other combinations for a pretty decorative detail.

 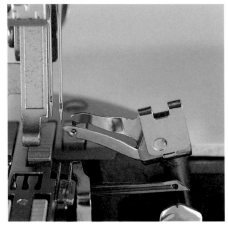 

Another attachment usually considered standard with the machine is the quilt guide. The bar slides nicely into the presser foot shank and can be used for any number of reasons: even chain stitching, quilting, or topstitching to name just a few.

The 2-thread converter fits easily over the upper looper blocking the eye of the looper for 2-thread stitch formations. Standard equipment on many models of machine, this 2-thread converter affords you numerous stitch possibilities.

Another accessory that can be very useful in your serging is the curve guide set. This accessory is easily attached to the front of the machine with an attachment holder base and attachment holder. Use this set to serge a curved edge to a straight edge evenly. The curved edge is placed on the top level with the straight edge on the bottom level.

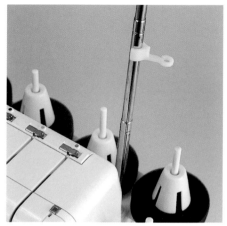

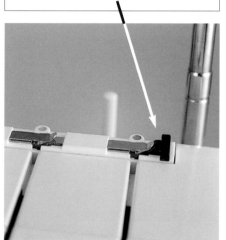

Review the many presser feet and attachments available for your machines with your sewing machine dealer. Some of the names may differ between brands but the techniques they perform remain the same. Learn the most you can about your machine so you will enjoy your sewing machine and serger more.

Many manufacturers provide snap-on thread guides to be used with decorative threads. It is also recommended that heavier threads be threaded through the thread guide antenna rather than through the slot.

Tension release guides can also be used on your machine to allow heavier threads flow through the serger easier. These guides help you control the tensions more easily.

Let's DECORATE

Sewing for your home can be gratifying

and fun. Most sewing or serger projects

are easy as most home decorating is

just sewing straight seams. By using the

many accessories available for both

machines, decorating your home can be

fast and painless!

SIMPLE CHAIR COVER

Transform any folding or occasional chair into a simple room accent by adding an easy-to-serge chair cover. Quickly hem the edges with the cover hem stitch.

TIP

- Guide the fabric through the hemming guide evenly. Gently roll the hem to the underside, keeping the edge even with the guide.

- It is easiest to hem on flat sections first then sew any side seams.

1 Cut fabric based on measurements of chair of choice. Piece fabrics if necessary to create one long section for front and back. Cut separate pieces for sides.

3 Position long section on chair. Mark placement for side sections and ties. Plan three ties down each back side and two along chair legs.

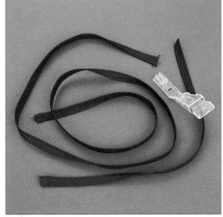

2 Using the Cover Hem attachment , guide 1" hem through machine along bottom edges on front/back section and sides. Hem side edges on side pieces similarly. Do not hem sides of long section yet.

4 Cut 1⅛"-wide bias strips from coordinating fabric for ties. Using Beltloop foot and Cover Hem Wide, make ties. Cut to desired length.

5 Turn under 1" hem along sides of long section. With wrong sides together, pin side sections and ties at marks. Serge side seams with cover hem encasing side sections in seam.

MATERIALS

- Decorator fabric of choice: measure and add together — from floor to seat; depth of seat; height of back; top of back to floor; add sides — floor to seat; allow for 1" seam allowances and hems
- Optional: 1 yard of coordinating fabric for ties
- Polyester sewing thread

SERGER SET-UP

Stitch Selection: ■ Cover Hem Wide or Cover Hem

Attachments: ■ Cover Hem foot; Beltloop foot

Thread: ■ Polyester sewing thread

Tensions: ■ Cover Hem Wide (CL—1.0, CN—6.0, LN—6.0)

Length: ■ Normal setting

Differential Feed: ■ Normal setting

SERGER MEMORY BOXES

Design a decorative memory box using a variety of serger stitches
and details. Be as creative as you like in serging this family heirloom.

TIP

- When making Deco Braid, hold soutache from the back of foot to get started.

- Remember to hold the rolled hem chain straight out the back of the foot, keeping even tension on the threads when making chain for tassels. This prevents "hiccups" in the chain stitch.

1 Measure diameter and height of sides of box and top. Cut fabric accordingly allowing for turn at bottom and top edges. Glue pieces in place. Hold with clothes pins until dry.

2 Trace two top pieces from pattern tracing paper. Divide one pattern piece into sections adding ¼" seam allowance to

inner edges. Flatlock sections with Pearl Crown Rayon, wrong sides together. With second pattern piece on flatlocked sections, trim to size. Glue to top of box.

3 For bow or flower, cut strip of fabric 1½" wide by 3 feet. Thread fishing line through hole on standard presser foot and serge edges with rolled hem. Form bow or roll into flower and glue in place.

4 Attach taping foot and tape and cord guide to machine. Thread soutache through guide and under foot. Using the Deco Braid setting, serge with Glamour thread creating decorative trim for top edge. Glue in place.

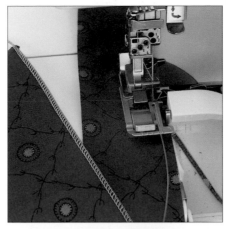

5 For round box, gather both edges of 2½"-wide strip of fabric with gathering foot. Glue to top, wrapping strip around edges. Follow above procedure for decorative trim; braid three tapes together and glue to edges of strip. Create rolled hem chains with Glamour and Woolly Nylon™ threads for tassels. Glue buttons, trinkets and tassels to tops.

MATERIALS

- 1 yard each of three to four coordinating fabrics
- Assorted shaped cardboard boxes from craft store
- Nylon fishline (30 lb.)
- Pearl Crown Rayon, Woolly Nylon™, Glamour threads to contrast or coordinate
- Soutache braid to coordinate
- Assorted buttons or trinkets
- Fabric glue
- Pattern tracing paper

SERGER SET-UP

Stitch Selections: ■ Flatlock 3; Deco Braids K2 (Elna ProCard A2); Rolled hem 3; Gathering (Elna ProCard 1); Wrapped Edge (Elna ProCard 4)

Attachments: ■ Gathering foot; Taping foot and Tape and Cord Guide

Threads: ■ UL—Pearl Crown Rayon for Flatlock 3; UL—Glamour for Deco Braids K2

Tensions: ■ Flatlock 3 (UL—2.0, LL—7.0, RN—1.0); Deco Braids K2 (UL—1.0, LL—4.0, RN—4.0); Rolled Hem 3 (UL—2.0, LL—6.0, RN—4.0); Gathering (UL—2.0, LL—2.0, RN—5.0, LN—6.0)

Lengths: ■ 4.0 for gathering; 2.0 for Deco Braids K2

Differential Feed: ■ 2.0 for gathering

PEARLY BATHROOM

Create a "pearly" rendition shower curtain and window valance for your bathroom. Hem the edges professionally and easily with either a sturdy, serged blindhem or flatlock stitch for durability.

1 Cut fabric according to measurements in Materials box which includes: 4½" for header; 4" for hem; and 6" which allows for each side hem.

2 Fold down top edge 2¼" twice for header. Fold header back on itself, placing fabric under presser foot with folded edge against guide. Adjust guide so needle barely catches fold of fabric. Blindhem

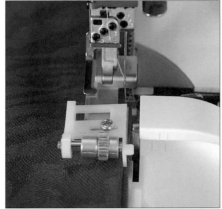

header in place. Add grommets or machine-made buttonholes, evenly spaced, to header for shower hooks. For valance, repeat above hemming on header then measure down 1" from top and straight stitch, making casing for rod.

3 For a double-folded flatlock hem, turn up 2" then 2" again, along bottom edge. Fold hem back on itself lining up folded edges under foot against guide. Lower blade to avoid cutting fabric. Flatlock hem in place. Open out flat.

4 Turn back each side 1½" and 1½" again for side hems. Fold fabric back on itself and serge in place. Embellish with pearl buttons in design of choice using the button sewing foot.

TIP

- A 2- or 3-thread flatlock stitch will work equally well on side or bottom hems.

- Use a 2-thread flatlock for sheer fabrics.

MATERIALS

- Fabric of choice:
  width = shower rod + 12";
  length = distance from top of rod to desired length + 8½"
- Pearl buttons
- Grommet kit

SERGER SET-UP

Stitch Selections:	Blindhem (Elna ProCard 3) or Flatlock 2 or 3
Attachments:	Blindhem foot, 2-thread converter for Flatlock 2
Thread:	Polyester serger thread
Tensions:	Blindhem (UL—2.0, LL—2.0, LN—4.0); Flatlock 2 (LL—5.0, RN—1.0); Flatlock 3 (UL—2.0, LL—7.0, RN—1.0)
Length:	2.0 – 2.5
Differential Feed:	Normal setting

SWEET DREAMS PILLOWS

Enjoy sweet dreams upon specially designed potpourri pillows.
Monograms, words, or even delicate embroidery is a perfect embellishment for the top.

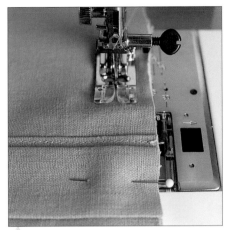

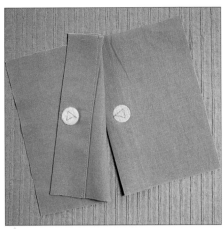

1 Cut one linen and one fleece piece 8" x 11"; one linen 8" x 8½"; and remaining linen piece 8" x 7½". Using two smaller pieces, press under 1" and then same again along 8½" and 7½" sides. Stitch along inside folded edge.

2 Overlap smaller pieces by 1"; baste to hold in place forming pillow back.

3 Attach Velcro™ brand dot to each flap.

MATERIALS

- 1½ yards each of pastel shade linen
- 1½ yards fleece
- 2 spools coordinating rayon embroidery thread
- 1 spool bobbin–weight thread
- 1 yard muslin
- Double needle appropriate for pintuck foot
- Buckwheat hulls, potpourri, or batting

SEWING MACHINE SET-UP

Stitch Selections:	▪ Outline quilting embroidery design; monogram; or letters of choice
Attachments:	▪ Darning or embroidery foot; 5-groove pintuck foot
Thread:	▪ Decorative thread for needle(s)
Lengths:	▪ Preset for embroidery
Stitch Width:	▪ Preset for embroidery
Needle Position:	▪ Preset for embroidery
Feed Dogs:	▪ Lowered for embroidery and monogram patterns; raised for pintucks

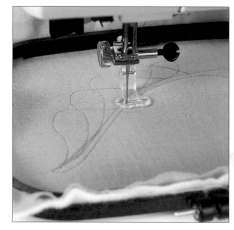

4 Allowing for 1" flange, center outline quilting design on linen top. Layer over fleece and insert into embroidery frame. Attach to machine and stitch.

5 With right sides together, using ½" seams, stitch front to back sections. Turn and press. Measure in 1" for flange. Stitch on markings. Make muslin inner pillows to fit. Stuff with buckwheat hulls, potpourri, or batting and slipstitch closed.

6 As a design alternative, attach pintuck foot and guide to machine. Thread cord under foot. Mark in 2½" from cut edge on top.

7 Using mark as a guide stitch three rows of pintucks on pillow top, one inside the other.

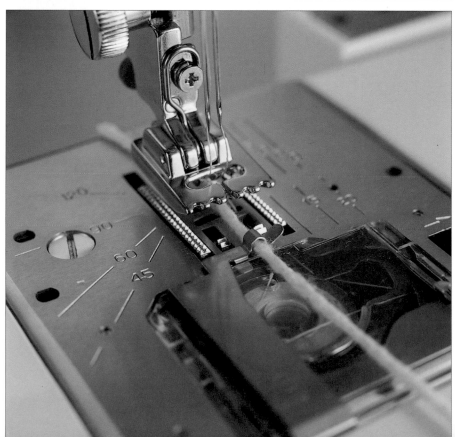

7 Center monogram design on pillow top. Layer linen over fleece; insert in embroidery frame and stitch.

8 For third pillow, center and stitch word in lettering style of choice. Finish all pillows as in step 5 above.

TIP

- Check your sewing machine instruction manual for the threading pattern for double needles. Place one thread on each side of the tension disc.

RECYCLED SWEATERS

Cut and flatlock old sweater pieces together, exposing the ladder-side
of the stitch. Weave decorative threads or strips of Ultrasuede™ for color accent.

MATERIALS

- Five old, worn sweaters
- Four 9" x ¼" Ultrasuede™ fabric, ribbon, or decorative trim strips
- 16" pillow form
- Large-eyed needle or flat bodkin
- Seam sealant

SERGER SET-UP

Stitch Selections:	Flatlock 3; 4-thread overlock
Attachments:	Knife lowered
Thread:	Polyester serger thread
Tensions:	Flatlock 3 (UL—2.0, LL—7.0, RN—1.0)
Length:	2.0 or slightly longer
Differential Feed:	Normal setting

1 Cut four 8¼"-square sections from ribbed edge of each sweater. Cut one 16½" square for back of pillow.

2 Expose ladder-side of flatlock stitch by placing two squares right sides together. Line edge of sweater knit along edge of presser foot and serge. Turn over and flatten out flatlock sections along seamline. Repeat with remaining two squares.

3 Thread large-eyed needle or flat bodkin with Ultrasuede™ strip. Weave through ladder-side of flatlock stitch alternating every two rows or create different weaving pattern.

4 Serge two sections together with flatlock stitch matching centers. Open top out flat, adjusting flatlock.

5 Weave Ultrasuede™ strips through flatlock ladder on remaining two sections, hiding ends in the center.

6 Using 4-thread serger stitch, serge front to back, right sides together, at sides leaving ribbed ends open.

7 Insert pillow form pinning along open ends. Using a narrow zig-zag, stitch along open ends. Clip ribbing to create fringe.

TIP

- For a joining seam such as this, use a stronger 3-thread flatlock rather than a 2-thread stitch.

- Use a heavier, decorative thread in the lower looper for added detail to the flatlock.

- Adjust your differential feed if necessary while you are serging to prevent rippling or stretching of the sweater knits.

CLASSY COVERS

Match your decor with piped or ruffled stool
covers. A serged elasticized band holds the covers in place.

1 Layer fleece and fabric, fabric side down, on serger. Using Quilt Stitch, quilting guide and nylon filament thread, quilt stool tops.

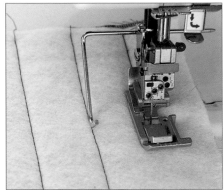

TIP

- On some machines, the elastic will be encased, while on others the stitching will be through the elastic.

- Test the elastic ratio on a sample before serging the finished project.

2 Using sewing machine, stitch purchased decorative cording to top edge. Or gather single thickness along long edge of ruffled band using gathering foot on serger. With right sides together, serge short ends, making circle. Turn up hem 1" along unfinished edge. Blindhem in place. Serge ruffle to top.

3 Thread elastic through elastic gatherer. Attach gatherer to front of multi-purpose foot pulling elastic under back of foot. Tighten screw to adjust gathering ratio. Adjust elastic gatherer support so elastic is not cut while serging. Serge over elastic only, about ½"–1", using 3-thread overlock stitch.

4 Place fabric band under foot, serge, trimming ¼" of fabric from edge. Adjust elastic tension while stitching.

5 Attach elasticized band to ruffled or corded top with 4-thread serger stitch or

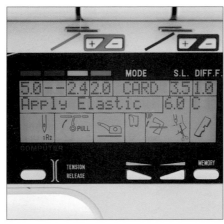

MATERIALS

- Fabric yardage:
  Stool top = measure around stool top adding ½" to each side for seam allowance; ruffle width = 4" by (stool top dimensions x 2);
  fabric band = 4½" by (stool top dimensions + 5")
- ¼" elastic
- Nylon filament thread
- Fleece: yardage based on top measurements
- Purchased decorative cording: yardage based on top measurements

SERGER SET-UP

Stitch Selections: ■ Gathering Stitch (Elna ProCard 1); Quilt Stitch (Elna ProCard A3); Blindhem (Elna ProCard 3); Apply Elastic (Elna ProCard 3)

Attachments: ■ Multi-purpose foot and 7.5mm elastic gatherer; Gathering foot; Blindhem foot, Quilting Guide; 2-thread converter; Rolled hem stitch finger exposed for Quilt Stitch

Threads: ■ Polyester serger thread; Quilt Stitch (LL—nylon) filament

Tensions: ■ Gathering (UL—2.0, LL—2.0, RN—5.0, LN—6.0); Quilt Stitch (LL—1.0, LN—4.0); Blindhem (UL—2.0, LL—2.0, LN—4.0); Apply Elastic (UL—2.4, LL—2.0, LN—5.0)

Length: ■ 3.0 – 4.0

Differential Feed: ■ Normal setting

TASSELED RUNNER

Use a printed fabric to help you create your quilting designs. This table runner can be used on either side as the stitching shows on the reverse side with decorative thread.

TIP

- When outline quilting with different weights of thread on top and bottom, adjust upper tension slightly, if necessary, so bobbin thread doesn't show on top.

1 Cut one piece, 37" x 18", from each fabric and fleece. Angle ends if desired.

2 Layer pieces of fabric, wrong sides together, and top with layer of fleece. Using ½" seam allowance, seam sides leaving opening for turning. Trim seams, turn and press.

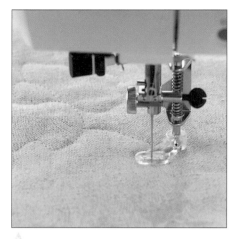

3 Slipstitch opening closed. Edgestitch around all sides.

4 Thread the machine with nylon filament thread in the needle and metallic thread on the bobbin. Following the pattern on the printed fabric, with feed dogs dropped and darning foot attached, outline the design with small stitches. The metallic thread on the bobbin will create a pattern on the solid fabric.

5 Create lengths of rolled hem chain using the serger and heavy decorative thread in the upper looper. Wrap chain around cardboard to make tassels. Attach tassels to each end of runner.

MATERIALS

- 1 yard each of two coordinating fabrics — one print, one solid
- 1 yard of fleece
- Nylon filament thread
- Metallic thread
- Heavy decorative thread for tassel
- Polyester sewing thread

SEWING MACHINE SET-UP

Stitch Selections:	- Straight stitch
Attachments:	- Darning foot
Thread:	- Nylon filament in needle; metallic on bobbin
Stitch Length:	- N/A for outline quilting
Stitch Width:	- 0
Needle Position:	- Center
Feed Dogs:	- Lowered for outline quilting

TIERED TABLECLOTHS

Layer two or more circular cloths to add a special decorative touch to a room. Gather sheer fabric into a short topper with shiny rayon tassels for a finishing detail.

TIP

- Some decorator fabrics are available in 110"+ widths eliminating the need to piece and seam for circular toppers.

- To finish gathering a ruffle to a circular piece, remove the top layer of fabric from the gathering foot approximately 2" from the end and hold taut while stitching.

- Ruffles can be cut on crosswise grain on soft fabrics and gather nicely.

1 For bottom layer, cut and piece fabric to achieve desired circular width.

3 Cut sheer fabric for top layer. Cut 4¼"- wide piece for ruffle allowing two times circumference for gathering.

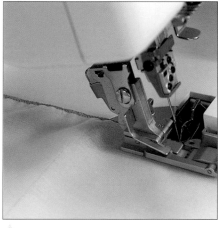

2 Turn up 1½" hem. Fold hem back on itself; place under foot with fold against guide on foot. Adjust guide to ensure a "blind" hem.

4 Finish one edge of ruffle using 2-thread rolled hem and metallic Woolly Nylon™ thread.

5 Using curve guide and gathering foot, place fabric to be gathered on bottom and the flat fabric on top in slot of foot. Serge with Gathering Stitch.

MATERIALS

- Fabric yardage:
  Undercloth = diameter of top + (drop to floor X 2) + 1½" (for hem); Ruffled cloth = diameter of top + (desired drop X 2) + 4¼" (for ruffle)

- Polyester serger thread; Metallic Woolly Nylon™

- Optional: tassels

SERGER SET-UP

Stitch Selections:
- Gathering Stitch (Elna ProCard 1); Blindhem (Elna ProCard 3); Woolly Rolled 2 (Elna ProCard 4)

Attachments:
- Gathering foot, Blindhem foot; Curve guide with attachment holder base and attachment holder; 2-thread converter and Rolled hem finger exposed for Woolly Rolled 2

Thread:
- LL—Metallic Woolly Nylon™ for Woolly Rolled 2

Tensions:
- Gathering Stitch (UL—2.0, LL—2.0, RN—5.0, LN—6.0); Blindhem (UL—2.0, LL—2.0, LN—4.0); Wooly Rolled 2 (LL—0.6, RN—6.6)

Length:
- Longest length for gathering

Differential Feed:
- Normal setting

BELTLOOP PILLOWS

Accent pillows or pillow covers are simple to create using the Beltloop foot
and the Cover Hem Stitch. Color and design are yours to decide.

1 Cut 19" squares from all fabrics. For pillow cover, cut 1⅛" bias strips for tabs.

2 Thread bias strip and ¼" elastic through Beltloop foot. Serge slowly guiding elastic through center of foot with stitch encasing elastic. Cut bias strips into eight - 4" lengths.

3 With wrong sides together, serge two opposite sides of 19" square with 4–thread stitch. Press, turn right side out. Fold to wrong side 1" hem on open ends. Pin raw ends of bias strips under hem equidistant apart. Serge in place using Cover Hem and 1" Hem guide.

MATERIALS

- For 18" pillow: 1 yard of print fabric for pillow cover; 1 yard each of 3–4 coordinating fabrics for "slashed" pillow
- 18" pillow form
- 8 decorative buttons for pillow cover
- 1¼ yards of ¼" elastic
- Polyester sewing thread

SERGER SET-UP

Stitch Selections:	▪ Cover Hem Wide, Cover Hem, Triple Cover Hem, Chain stitch; 4–thread stitch
Attachments:	▪ Beltloop foot; Cover Hem foot and 1" Hem guide
Thread:	▪ Polyester sewing thread
Tensions:	▪ Cover Hem Wide (CL—1.0, CN—6.0, LN—6.0); Cover Hem (CL—1.0, CN—6.0, RN—6.0); Chain stitch (CL—2.0, CN—4.0); Triple Cover Hem (CL—1.0, CN—6.0, LN—6.0, RN—6.0)
Length:	▪ Normal setting
Differential Feed:	▪ Normal setting

■ Wash and dry "slashed" pillow cover a number of times to allow fabric to fray at slashes.

■ Try other beltloop designs such as cross-hatching the strips on a pillow top, using several beltloop strips to make tassels at the corners, or using elasticized beltloops to ruch the pillow top.

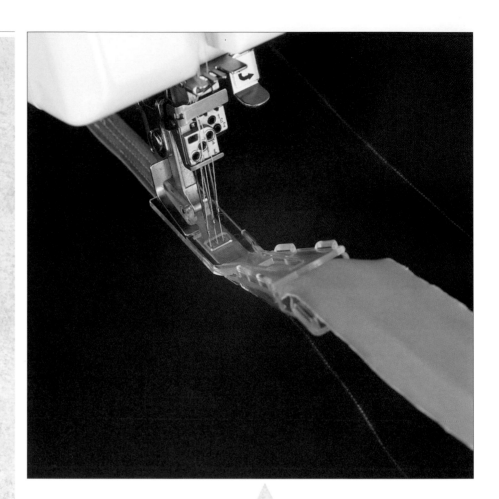

4 For "slashed" pillow, layer 3 different colors of fabric together. Place marks diagonally across center on top layer approximately 2"–3" apart. Chain-stitch "baste" if desired across layers.

5 Cut 1⅛" bias strips of contrasting color. Using Triple Cover Hem, serge bias strips across layers of fabric, following marks.

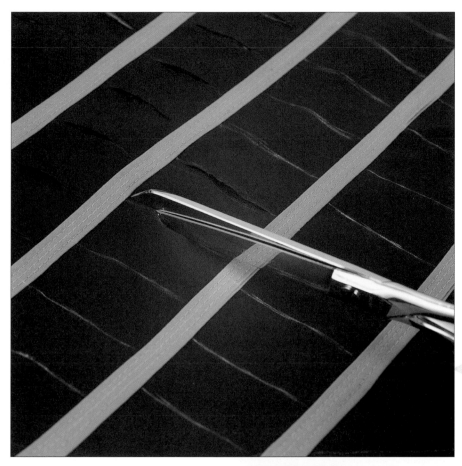

6 Make "slashes" through all layers of fabric between bias strips about 1½" apart.

7 Serge fourth layer to back of top. This color will show through slashes.

8 With wrong sides together, serge three sides of pillow together. Wash and dry cover. Turn and stuff. Whipstitch closed.

STARS GALORE

Appliquéd stars shine across this easy–to–make banner and windsock. Enjoy their design simplicity as the wind flutters through them on your porch or deck.

MATERIALS

- 1 yard each of two colors of rainwear fabric
- Grommets and pliers
- Polyester sewing thread
- 25" ring for windsock
- 2 yards of nylon cord for windsock

SEWING MACHINE SET-UP

Stitch Selections:	Straight and zig zag stitches
Attachments:	6mm hemmer foot, appliqué foot
Thread:	Polyester sewing thread
Stitch Length:	2–2.5mm; satin stitch
Stitch Width:	0; 1.5–2.5mm
Needle Position:	Center
Feed Dogs:	Raised

1 For banner, cut fabric 20" x 35". For wind-sock, measure circumference of ring and , adding 1" for seam allowance, cut measure-ment x 15"; cut 12 - 14 streamers 2½" x length desired.

2 Finish side edges of banner and edges of streamers using hemmer foot. To begin, double-fold narrow edge and place under foot. Taking a couple stitches, leave needle down and guide fabric into roll of foot. Holding fabric straight in front of foot, stitch letting fabric slide through foot.

3 For banner turn down top edge ½", then 3½" again. Straight stitch to hem forming casing. Finish bottom of banner with hemmer foot as above.

4 Trace star patterns found on page 120 on contrasting fabric. With straight stitch, stitch stars to banner in pleasing pattern. Stitch stars to windsock while piece is still flat.

5 Satin stitch over straight stitches around edges of stars. Taper zig zag stitch at all points.

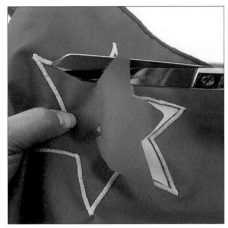

6 Trim base fabric from the back under each star being careful not to clip stars.

7 To finish windsock, with wrong sides together, seam short ends. Fold seam allowances together to one side. Stitch ¼" away from seam making mock flat-fell seam. Trim close to stitching.

8 Finish top and bottom edges on serg-er with 3– or 4–thread stitch. Wrap top edge over ring and stitch casing.

9 Fold up bottom edge ½". Pin stream-ers one next each other around edge. Straight stitch in place.

ELEGANT NECKROLL

Ruching adds a touch of texture to this simple but elegant designer neckroll.
Add quick serger techniques and your results will command "oohs" and "aahs".

MATERIALS

- ¾ yard each of two coordinating fabrics
- One package purchased piping
- Two 1" self-covered buttons
- Medium-size cording for gathered ends
- Fiber- or down-filled neck roll form
- Optional: tassels

SERGER SET-UP

Stitch Selections:
- Gathering Stitch (Elna ProCard 1); Blindhem (Elna ProCard 3); 4-thread overlock; 3-thread overlock

Attachments:
- Gathering foot; Blindhem foot

Thread:
- Polyester serger thread

Tensions:
- Gathering (UL—2.0, LL—2.0, RN—5.0, LN—6.0); Blindhem (UL—2.0, LL—2.0, LN—4.0)

Length:
- 4.0 for gathering

Differential Feed:
- 2.0 for gathering

1 Divide length of pillow into three equal parts. Add 1" for seam allowances and cut three pieces from fabrics. Measure diameter of pillow. Cut two rectangular end pieces, the diameter + 1" by radius + 1½".

2 With gathering foot, gather long edges of single layer of center fabric. Serge gathered edges between remaining fabric sections with 4-thread stitch. Create cylinder and serge long edge together.

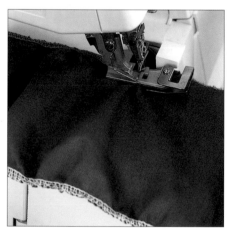

3 Attach purchased piping to each end with sewing machine overlapping ends for continuous piping. Serge end pieces into circles and stitch to piped sections.

4 To make casing, fold back hem 1" along end pieces. Blindhem in place leaving small opening for cord.

5 Thread bodkin or large-eyed needle with cord; insert in casing. Gather and tie ends. Cover buttons and attach over gathered ends.

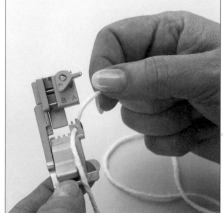

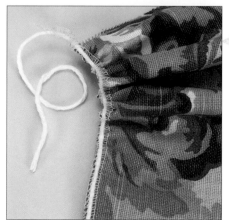

TIP

• To increase the gathering on heavier fabrics, lower the pressure control on the presser foot or serge over the stitches a second time.

• Increase the needle tensions or pull the needle threads for tighter gathers.

6 Optional method of gathering pillow ends: Thread cord through hole on standard serger foot or through hole on support plate of multi-purpose foot.

7 Using a wide 3-thread stitch, serge over cord creating a thread casing. Gather cord to fit. Finish as above.

TRIMMED CHERRY VALANCE

Serge up a pretty bias-trimmed valance with a deco-edge in little or no time.
Complete the scene with a complementary tablecloth and matching embroidered napkins.

1 Cut valance panel according to measurements. Serge-finish top edge with 3-thread stitch. Turn down top edge 1½" plus width of rod plus ½". At top, mark down 1½"; again at rod width plus ¼". Straight-stitch at marks.

2 Cut strips of bias 1⅜" wide. Insert into tape guide and under foot. Adjust guide placement and chain-stitch slowly. Place fabric, right side up, under tape and continue stitching.

3 Cut contrasting bands according to measurements. With wrong sides together, serge short edges together for sides and bottom. Using Deco-Overlock 3, serge decorative edge along one long edge.

4 Under standard serger foot, layer unfinished edge of contrasting band, right side up, under trimmed panel with trimmed edge up. Serge with 4-thread stitch. Repeat on side bands. Press seam down. Miter corners.

5 Bring decorative edge up over stitching on front of panel. Straight-stitch in place along edge. Follow same procedure for tablecloth. Cut napkins and with a 2- or 3-thread rolled hem, finish edges.

TIP

- Using either a 5-thread or chain stitch will determine the width of the bias trim exposed when using the tape guide.

- Embellish your napkins with a decorative embroidery design.

MATERIALS

- Fabric of choice: width = 2 x width of window; length = of choice + 3" for header + 2 x width of rod + 1" minus 3½"; 54" x 72" finished size of tablecloth
- Contrasting band: width = 2 x width of window by 4"; length = same as above by 4"; tablecloth: width = 4 pieces x 54" by 4"; length = 4 pieces 72" x 4"; napkins: 18½" squares
- ½ yard contrasting bias trim
- 2 spools of Pearl Crown Rayon, matching or contrasting
- Optional: lining

SERGER SET-UP

Stitch Selections:	Deco-Overlock 3 (Elna ProCard); Chain Stitch; Rolled Hem 2 or 3
Attachments:	Tape guide, Attachment Holder Base and Attachment Holder
Threads:	UL and LL—Pearl Crown Rayon for Deco-Overlock 3; UL—Woolly Nylon™ for Rolled Hem 3
Tensions:	Deco-Overlock 3 (UL—1.0, LL—3.6, LN—4.4); Chain Stitch (CL—2.0, CN—4.0) Rolled Hem 3 (UL—2.0, LL—6.0, RN—4.0)
Lengths:	3.0 for Deco-Overlock 3 and Chain Stitch; 1.0 for Rolled Hem 3
Differential Feed:	Normal setting

Let's DRESS UP

Be creative when sewing for yourself,

your family, or friends. Learn more about

the accessories that fit your machines,

utilize the many new exciting threads

available, and try stitching on some new

fabrics. Stamp, embroider, tuck, or fuse

to your hearts content!

CLASSIC BAGS

Antique-looking fabrics are the perfect partners for these handy little bags. Make all variations as gifts and practice using your blindhem or edgestitching foot.

1 Using the pattern on page 121, cut two pieces from fabric and two from lining. Mark pieces according to pattern.

2 With right sides together, stitch side seams of fabric and lining.

3 Place lining inside outer fabric right sides together. Stitch along top edge. Press seam to one side.

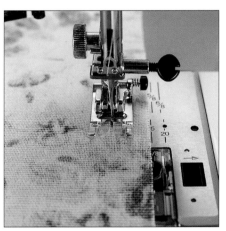

MATERIALS

- ½ yard of fabric
- ½ yard of lining fabric
- 1 yard of 1"–wide single–fold bias or twill tape
- 1 ½ yards of cording
- 1 yard each of flat and gathered lace trim (optional)

SEWING MACHINE SET-UP

Stitch Selections:	▪ Straight stitch
Attachments:	▪ Blindhem or edgestitching foot
Threads:	▪ Polyester sewing thread
Stitch Lengths:	▪ 2–2.5mm
Stitch Width:	▪ 0
Needle Position:	▪ Slightly to right or left of center for edgestitching
Feed Dogs:	▪ Raised

4 Stitch flat lace to top edge using blind-hem or edgestitching foot and positioning needle just inside trim edge.

5 With right sides together, stitch bottom seam of outer fabric.

6 Center bottom seam and match edges. Stitch box corners. Finish raw edges of lining with 3– or 4–thread serger stitch. With wrong sides together, repeat steps 5 and 6 on lining. Turn lining to inside.

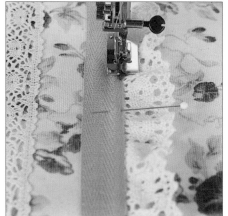

7 Pin twill or bias tape to outside through all layers at markings. Insert gathered lace under bottom edge. Stitch edges leaving ends open at side seams.

TIP

- For edgestitching, move the needle position to the right or left of center. Place the blade on the foot next to the edge of the fabric and stitch.

- Make bias strips easily with a bias tape maker. Guide the fabric through the appropriately sized tape maker and just press.

8 Cut two lengths of cord for bag straps. Thread cord through casing looping in the opposite directions at the sides.

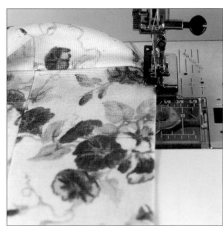

9 Add a pocket and bias trim at the top edge as an alternative detail. Cut one pocket piece 7" x 5". Turn under ½" on each side and 1" down from top; press. With blind-hem or edgestitching foot, stitch pocket to outer fabric at marks before stitching side seams as in step 2.

12 Form a box-like bag by edgestitching at four sides. Fold layers together from bottom to top and stitch.

10 With right sides together, stitch side, bottom, and box corner seams on both outer fabric and lining. With wrong sides together place lining inside outer fabric matching upper raw edges. Baste top edges together.

11 Cut bias 2" bias strips. Fold raw edges to center, press. Fold in half and press. Wrap top edge with bias strips and edgestitch in place.

PEARL-EDGED SHAWL

Quickly serge an elegant 45"-square shawl by adding pearls along the edge and flatlocking a 4" border. Add a serger tassel to the corner for a finishing touch.

TIP

- When flatlocking pearls to the middle of the fabric, the needle should just catch the edge of the fold so the pearls lie flat when the flatlock is opened.

1 Cut a true 45" square of fabric. Draw a placement line 4" from outer edge of square. Adjust serger for Pearl Flat 2 stitch and attach pearl foot and needle plate.

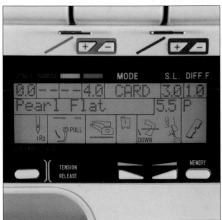

2 Place pearls under foot. Fold fabric, wrong sides together, along placement line and place under foot next to pearls. Take first few stitches by hand holding pearls from behind to avoid puckering. Adjust stitch length so stitches fall between pearls.

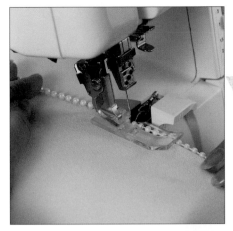

3 At corners, release tensions and pull threads and pearls slightly to the back. Pivot fabric and pearls to next side, adjusting fold in fabric. Hold pearls and move foot along placement line until resting flat on fabric. Continue serging. Tack loose pearls at corners by hand.

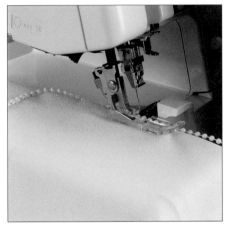

4 Either finish the hem edge with a narrow 3-thread stitch or adjust for 2-thread rolled hem. Place pearls and fabric under foot as before and serge. Turn corners as above. Add tassel to corner(s) if desired.

MATERIALS

- 45" square of fine crepe fabric
- 10 yards of 3mm pearls or beads to match or contrast
- Metallic Woolly Nylon™ thread

SERGER SET-UP

Stitch Selection: ■ Pearl Flat 2 (Elna ProCard 5)

Attachments: ■ 2-thread converter; Pearl foot and/or needle plate

Thread: ■ LL—Metallic Woolly Nylon™

Tensions: ■ Pearl Flat 2 (LL—4.0; RN—0.0)

Length: ■ Based on size of pearls or beads between 2.5 and 4.0

Differential Feed: ■ Normal setting

REVERSIBLE APRONS

Practice your edge-finishing techniques using versatile Woolly Nylon™
thread on cook and helper aprons. Add a Teflon™-coated fabric mitt to the mix.

1 Cut two apron pieces each from coordinating fabrics from patterns on page 122. For adult apron, cut eight 30" x 2" pieces for ties and two 17" x 9" pieces for pockets. For child apron, cut eight 25" x 2" pieces for ties and two 11" x 6" pieces for pockets. For mitt, cut three of fabric, two of fleece, and one of Teflon™-coated fabric.

2 Serge-finish all edges of each pocket piece. Straight-stitch pockets to apron fronts on placement lines. Divide each pocket in half; stitch through center.

3 With apron pieces wrong sides together and using wider Stretch Wrapped stitch for adult apron, stitch and trim ¼" along

each edge. Follow same procedure for child apron using narrower Wrapped Edge.

4 Serge ties, wrong sides together, along all edges with appropriate decorative stitch. Make four ties for each adult and child apron. Straight-stitch ties to top and sides at marks.

5 Layer fabric, fleece, and fabric for one side of mitt. Replace one fabric piece with Teflon™-coated fabric for other side. Stitch across bottom of each mitt section with Stretch Wrapped stitch.

6 Place mitt sections together with Teflon™-coated piece to outside. Following edge of fabric, stitch slowly with Stretch Wrapped stitch around remaining edges.

TIP

- When serging an acute, inside curve, trim away the seam allowance prior to stitching. Serge slowly straightening and adjusting the fabric under the foot around the curve.

- Use a Microtec needle, if necessary, for sewing on Teflon™-coated fabric.

MATERIALS

- 1 yard each of four coordinating fabrics
- ½ yard Teflon™-coated fabric
- ½ yard fleece
- Woolly Nylon™ thread to match or contrast
- Microtec needle
- Optional: rayon embroidery threads

SERGER SET-UP

Stitch Selections:
- Stretch Wrapped; Wrapped Edge (Elna ProCard 4)

Attachments:
- 2-thread converter; Rolled hem stitch finger exposed for Wrapped Edge stitch

Thread:
- LL—Woolly Nylon™

Tensions:
- Stretched Wrapped (LL—1.0; RN—4.0; LN—5.0)
- Wrapped Edge (LL—1.0; RN—4.6; LN—4.6)

Length:
- 2.0–2.5 or shorter

Differential Feed:
- Normal setting

SILKY BLOUSE AND COLLAR

Add a serger-embellished collar to a silky, jewel-neck blouse. Try a variety
of decorative techniques or experiment with unique threads for a fresh, new look.

1 Cut out blouse according to pattern. Stitch shoulder seams. Insert sleeves flat. Turn up 1" hems on sleeves and bottom edges. Using 1" Hem guide and Cover Hem Wide, finish sleeves and bottom edge of blouse.

2 With right sides together, serge side seams including sleeves using narrow 3–thread at ¼" seam allowance. Turn and press fabric around seams. With chain stitch, encase seam making French seams. Finish blouse according to pattern.

3 Trace collar onto tracing paper using pattern on page 123. Check collar piece against blouse pattern for fit. Adjust if necessary. Faintly trace collar outline placement lines on fabric.

MATERIALS

- Jewel-neck blouse pattern of choice
- Fabric based on pattern
- 1 yard of coordinating fabric for collar and lining
- 2–3 different metallic threads (e.g. Glamour)
- Pearl Crown Rayon
- Crochet cotton or fine cord

SERGER SET-UP

Stitch Selections:
- Chain stitch; Cover Hem; Cover Hem Wide; Narrow 3–thread

Attachments:
- Foot and Fagoting guide; Cover Hem foot and 1" Hem guide; Pintuck foot and Pintuck guide; Cording guide

Threads:
- CL—Pearl Crown Rayon or Glamour for Pintucks; CL—Glamour for Chain stitch

Tensions:
- Chain stitch (CL—2.0, CN—4.0); Cover Hem (CL—1.0, CN—6.0, LN—6.0); Cover Hem Wide (CL—1.0, CN—6.0, LN—6.0)

Length:
- 3.0 for Chain stitch

Differential Feed:
- Normal setting to "–" based on fabric

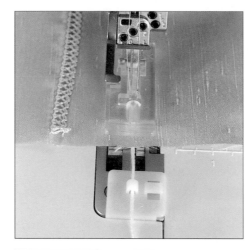

4 Thread Pearl Crown Rayon into chain looper. From wrong side, stitch uncorded pintucks using Pintuck foot only. From right side, thread narrow cord through Cording guide and serge pintucks on placement lines.

5 For fagoting turn under ½" along each cut edge at center front. Insert folded edges into each side of Fagoting guide. Lower needles into fabric and serge with Cover Hem. Stitch slowly.

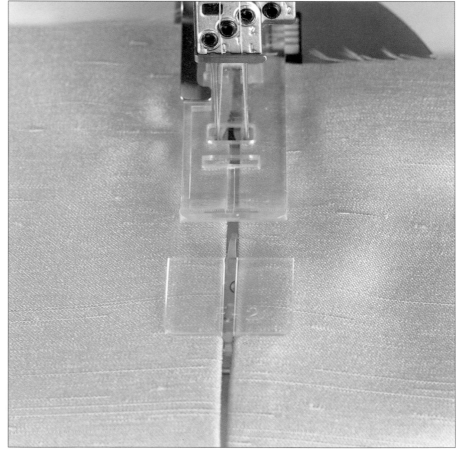

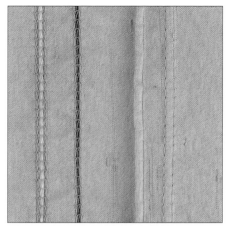

6 Add more rows of corded or uncorded pintucks as desired next to fagoting.

7 Using Glamour in the chainstitch looper, serge rows of chain stitch along placement lines found on pattern. Check embellished fabric against pattern and tracing. Cut out collar.

8 Cut second collor for lining. Stitch sides together leaving end open for turning. Turn, press, and slipstitch closed.

TIP

- The Pintuck guide raises the fabric without the help of a cord. Use it to make tiny tucks on crisp fabrics. Press the tucks to one side for a different appearance.

HATS AND ROSES

Velveteen or brocade and a few gathered fabric roses create elegance and charm on these pretty hats. Decorative threads add beautiful edge finishes and topstitching details.

MATERIALS

- Hat pattern of choice (e.g. Butterick 3342 or 4908; Vogue #9082 or 9333)
- Fabric yardage according to pattern
- Pearl Crown Rayon to match or contrast
- Woolly Nylon™
- Notions according to pattern

SERGER SET-UP

Stitch Selections:
- Deco-Overlock 3 (Elna ProCard 1) and Deco-Chain (Elna ProCard A2); or Wrapped Edge (Elna ProCard 4) and Wooly Rolled 3 (Elna ProCard 4)

Attachments:
- 2-thread converter; Rolled hem stitch finger exposed for Wrapped Edge and Deco-Chain

Threads:
- UL—Woolly Nylon™ for Rolled hem; LL—Pearl Crown Rayon thread for Deco-Overlock 3, Deco-Chain, and Wrapped Edge

Tensions:
- Deco-Overlock 3 (UL—1.0, LL—3.6, RN—4.4); Deco-Chain(LL—1.4, LN—4.0); Wrapped Edge (LL—1.0, RN—4.6, LN—4.6); Wooly Rolled 3 (UL—0.4, LL—8.0, RN—4.6)

Length:
- Appropriate to stitch; Deco-Chain at least 3.5

Differential Feed:
- Normal setting

1 For velveteen hat, cut fabric pieces according to pattern. Attach crown to top with 4-thread stitch or on sewing machine.

2 With wrong sides together, finish brim edge with Deco-Overlock 3 and Pearl Crown Rayon. Topstitch rows along wrong side of brim with Deco-Chain stitch using edge of presser foot as guide between rows.

3 Attach brim to crown according to pattern.

4 For visor variation, finish brim edge using Pearl Crown Rayon thread and Wrapped Edge stitch.

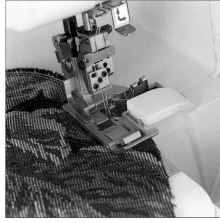

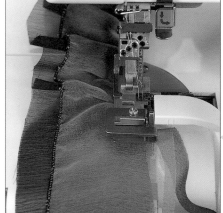

TIP

- Use at least a 3.5 or longer stitch length for the Deco-Chain. Serge from the wrong side of the fabric so the decorative thread of the chain is on the right side.

5 Finish remaining three edges of cap with rolled edge and Woolly Nylon™ thread.

6 For sheer gathered roses, gather two layers of sheer fabric together for interesting contrast.

7 Finish both edges of sheer strips with rolled hem and Woolly Nylon™ thread. Roll strips to make roses. Tack to brim with hand stitches.

BLANKET-STITCH VEST

Combine sewing machine and serger techniques to
create this blanket-stitch bound vest. Insert the zipper by serger too!

1 Cut vest fronts and back from felt and lining fabric.

2 Use lining fabric to design motif on vest fronts. Enlarge design on copy machine and trace on pattern tracing paper. Cut out motifs for pattern use.

3 Lay vest fronts on working surface and position motifs in pleasing manner. Cut motifs from various colored pieces of felt. Pin bottom layer pieces in position on vest fronts.

4 Select a narrow blanket stitch from your built-in sewing machine stitches. Carefully follow outline of bottom pieces with stitching.

5 Select 3-thread rolled hem using Pearl Crown Rayon in upper looper. Use over-lock thread in right needle and Woolly Nylon™ in lower looper. Lower cutting knife to avoid cutting thread. Hold thread ends to back of presser foot and begin serging. Continue holding rolled hem chain from back of foot and serge length desired. Make chains in a variety of colors.

6 Set serger for Deco-Chain. Thread chain looper with Pearl Crown Rayon. From wrong side, carefully make flower stamen on base fabric of flower. Stitch forward and pivot, leaving needle tip in fabric; stitch back. Stitch as many times as desired, back and forth.

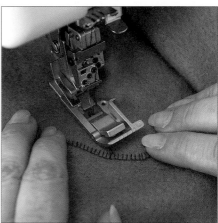

MATERIALS

- Vest pattern of choice (Adapt Great Copy pattern #835 to a vest)
- 1 yard of felt
- 1 yard cotton print for lining
- 8"x10" pieces of assorted colors of felt
- Numerous spools of Pearl Crown Rayon to match or contrast
- 18" separating zipper
- Two spools Woolly Nylon™ thread
- Polyester serger thread
- Matching polyester sewing machine thread

SERGER SET-UP

Stitch Selections:
- Blanket Stitch (Elna ProCard 3); Blindhem (Elna ProCard 3); Deco-Chain (Elna ProCard); Rolled Hem 3

Attachments:
- Blindhem foot for zipper application; Chainstitch foot; Rolled hem stitch finger cap exposed for Rolled hem and Deco-Chain; Disengage UL

Threads:
- UL and LL—Woolly Nylon™, LN— Pearl Crown Rayon for Blanket Stitch

Tensions:
- Blindhem (UL—2.0, LL—2.0, LN—4.0); Blanket Stitch (UL—8.0, LL—9.0, LN—by-pass tension); Deco-Chain (CL—1.4, CN—4.0); Rolled Hem 3 (UL—2.0, LL—6.0, RN—4.0)

Lengths:
- 4.0 for Blanket Stitch; 3.5 or longer for Deco-Chain

Differential Feed:
- Normal setting

7 Loop multi-colored chains together for flower center. Straight-stitch in place along bottom of base of motif. Stitching will be covered by next layer of flower motif.

8 Finish any unattached edges of outer layers of flower with narrow sewing-machine blanket stitch. Stack layers as desired for color and interest. Pin outer layers in place on flower covering thread chain ends. Attach with blanket stitch.

9 Place leaves and small buds in place and stitch as above.

10 With wrong sides together, lay felt and lining vest fronts and vest backs together. Treat each layer as one piece. Serge shoulder seams with 4-thread stitch.

11 Fold back ½" along each side of center front. Using basting tape, center zipper under opening. Open zipper completely. Fold each side of center front back on itself (like a blindhem). Position one side of zipper under blindhem foot; serge zipper in place. Repeat for other side.

12 Finish neckline and bottom edge with blanket stitch.

TIP

- Be sure to hold rolled hem chain straight out the back of the foot while chaining to avoid any "hiccups" in stitching.

- Use either the blindhem foot or the standard serger foot when applying the zipper. The bulk of the fabric and zipper will determine which foot to use.

- Adjust the blanket stitch with your fingernails if the needle thread is exposed.

FAGOTED SKIRT AND TOP

Beautiful fagoting is turned from a hand technique into a sewing machine technique quickly and easily. The guide separates the fabrics while the stitching bridges the gap.

MATERIALS

- Skirt and top pattern of choice
- Fabric yardage based on pattern
- Heavy decorative thread
- Rayon thread

SEWING MACHINE SET-UP

Stitch Selections:
- Fagoting, Patchwork, Multi-zig zag stitches

Attachments:
- Fagoting guides; Buttonhole foot; Button Sewing foot

Threads:
- Heavy decorative thread on bobbin; rayon thread in needle

Stitch Lengths:
- According to stitch

Stitch Width:
- According to stitch

Needle Position:
- According to stitch

Feed Dogs:
- Raised

TIP

- Feed band and skirt bottom evenly under foot. It may be necessary to slightly shift the band under the foot while sewing to keep the two fabrics even.

1 Cut fabric according to pattern, shortening skirt by 3½". Stitch side seams; finish waist band to choice. Clean-finish bottom edge with 3– or 4–thread serger stitch. Press up ½" along bottom edge.

2 Cut two strips for bottom of skirt 7" by width of skirt pattern. Stitch one side seam, right sides together. Fold strip in half, right sides together and stitch long side. Turn tube to right side, positioning seam in center of one side. Press. Stitch remaining side seam making fabric ring.

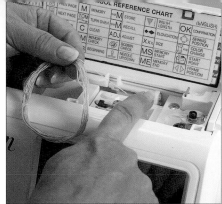

3 Carefully wind heavy decorative thread on bobbin. Hold decorative thread in one hand and fill bobbin evenly.

4 Matching side seams, loosely pin band to skirt bottom. Attach fagoting guide to machine. With right sides up, slide band over freearm followed by bottom skirt edge. Select stitch of choice and begin stitching while guiding fabric and band evenly under foot next to guide. The stitches create a web between the two fabrics.

5 Repeat fagoting down front band on top. Make buttonholes in band and attach buttons with the button sewing foot.

HEIRLOOM HANKIE

French hand-sewing techniques easily adapt to the serger. Use a finer 2-thread rolled hem on these delicate laces and fine linen fabric.

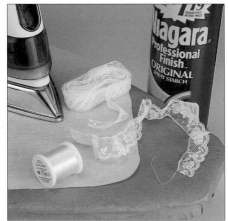

1 Determine size of finished hankie by measuring lampshade depth. Cut square from linen dividing into quarters lengthwise. Spray-starch linen and laces.

2 Place one-quarter piece of linen under blindhem foot and lace next to guide on top of fabric, adjusting guide so needle just pierces header of lace. Using 2-thread rolled hem, trim excess fabric from edge. Repeat for other side.

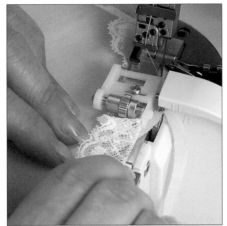

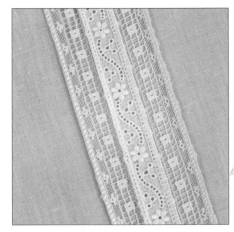

3 Serge lace to both sides of insertion embroidery with rolled hem. Serge to linen along both sides.

4 Pull gathering thread in header of edging lace. Pin to edge of hankie adjusting gathers. Following same procedure, serge with rolled hem to edge trimming excess fabric. Turn back ¼" of lace overlapping ends to finish.

MATERIALS

- ½ yard linen
- ½ yard embroidered insertion
- 1½ yard insertion lace
- 2 yards edging lace
- Rayon thread to match lace

SERGER SET-UP

Stitch Selection:	■ Rolled Hem 2
Attachments:	■ Blindhem foot; Rolled hem finger exposed
Thread:	■ UL—rayon thread
Tensions:	■ UL—4.0; RN—4.0
Length:	■ 1 or less
Differential Feed:	■ Normal setting

BATH WRAP, MITT & SLIPPERS

Serge up a bath wrap, mitt, and slippers using the bias binders. Wonderful
shower gifts, these bath accessories utilize a number of serger stitches.

TIP

- Cut one end of the bias strip at an angle for easier insertion into the bias binder.

- To finish bias binding around circular shape, trim bias tape 3″ longer than finished edge. Fold tape back and carefully feed into binder. Continue stitching over previous stitches. Run chain stitch off edge. Pick out unnecessary stitches from binding tape.

1 Measure around body above bustline with tape measure; add 8" for overlap. Cut rectangle of terry cloth this measurement by 28" long.

2 For front trim, cut 4½" wide by 28" strip of one fabric and 2½" by 28" strip of second. Fold each strip in half lengthwise and press.

3 Layer narrow strip and wide strip on left front edge of terry cloth 1" from edge. Serger layers using balanced 4-thread stitch. Turn to front and press.

4 Cut 2" bias strips from coordinating fabric. Press both edges to center. Using adjustable bias binder foot and chain stitch, insert tape into foot and stitch on tape first. Insert right front edge of terry cloth between layers of tape; continue serging.

MATERIALS

- 2½ yards of terry cloth fabric
- ½ to 1 yard each of three or four coordinating fabrics
- 1 yard of ½" elastic
- 6" hook and loop tape or 2 large hook and eyes
- ½ yard fleece for slippers

SERGER SET-UP

Stitch Selections:	■ Bias Binder (Elna ProCard A3); Chain Stitch; Blindhem (Elna ProCard 3)
Attachments:	■ Bias Binder foot, adjustable or Bias Binder Attachment; Blindhem foot
Thread:	■ Polyester sewing thread
Tensions:	■ Bias Binder (CL—1.0, CN—4.0); Chain Stitch (CL—2.0, CN—4.0) Blindhem (UL—2.0, LL—2.0, LN—4.0)
Lengths:	■ 3.5 for Bias Binder; 3.0 for Chain Stitch
Differential Feed:	■ Normal setting

5 Measure down 1½" from top edge, mark. Fold fabric along marks and then back on itself. With blindhem foot, serge, making casing along top. Measure in 8" from each edge along casing; mark. Insert elastic between marks. Try on wrap and adjust. Straight-stitch elastic ends at marks. Attach hook and loop strips or large hook and eyes to wrong side of casing at each side of upper edges. Adjust to fit.

6 Measure up 1½" for hem. Turn up fabric along marks and then back on itself. Serge with blindhem.

7 For mitt, cut two pieces from terry cloth using pattern "A" on page 124. Cut 2" bias strips of coordinating fabric. Press long edges of bias to center.

8 Finish bottom edge of each terry cloth piece using bias binder and chain stitch. Allowing 4" of bias tape at one end for loop, layer mitt pieces and serge bias tape to outer edge. Continue serging on tape only; fold back to edge and tack in place.

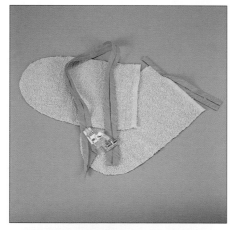

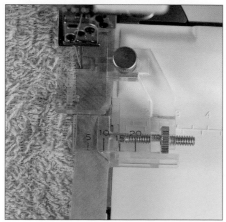

9 For slippers, using pattern "B" on page 124, measure foot against pattern. Enlarge if necessary. Cut two pieces from terry cloth, one from fleece. Cut two pieces from pattern "C" from coordinating fabric and one from fleece. Cut strip from second fabric, 3½" by 7½", and strip, 1¾" by 7½", from third fabric. Press strips in half.

10 Press both strips in half lengthwise. With wrong sides together, layer fabrics bottom to top in this order matching raw edges: fleece piece "C", lining piece "C", folded 1¾" strip, folded 3½" strip, and outer piece "C". Serge using 4-thread stitch. Press seam so coordinating band is exposed.

11 Layer fleece between sole pieces and place banded section on top matching outer edges. Using adjustable bias binder, stitch through all layers.

MAKE-UP ROLL

A great gift for a special friend, this serged make-up roll takes very little time to make. Coordinate it with the terry wrap, wash mitt, and slippers for an unbeatable combination.

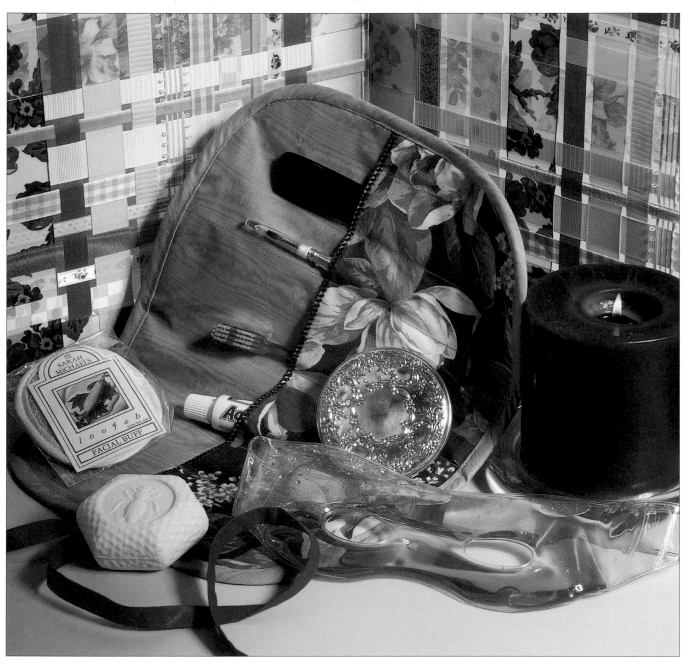

1 Cut 10" x 14" rectangles, one each from print, coordinating fabric for lining, vinyl, and fleece. Cut 5" x 14" from print for pocket. Round corners using small plate or curved edge.

2 Following manufacturers instructions, bond vinyl to right side of lining piece.

3 Using Pearl Crown Rayon and Deco-Overlock 3, serge top edge of pocket. With right side to wrong side, pin pocket to vinyl lining.

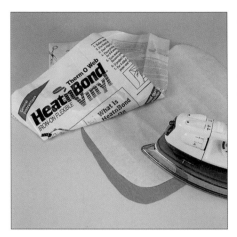

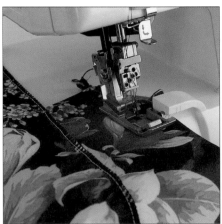

MATERIALS

- 1 yard of print fabric
- 1½ yards of coordinating lining fabric
- ½ yard of iron-on vinyl
- ½ yard fleece
- Pearl Crown Rayon
- Nylon filament thread

SERGER SET-UP

Stitch Selections:	■ Quilt Stitch (Elna ProCard A3); Deco-Overlock 3 (Elna ProCard 1); Bias Binder (Elna ProCard A3); Cover Hem Wide
Attachments:	■ Bias Binder foot, adjustable; Beltloop foot
Threads:	■ LL—Pearl Crown Rayon for Deco-Overlock 3; LN—nylon filament thread for Quilt Stitch
Tensions:	■ Quilt Stitch (CL—1.0, LN—4.0); Deco-Overlock 3 (UL—1.0, LL—3.6, RN—4.4); Bias Binder (CL—1.0, CN—4.0); Cover Hem Wide (CL—1.0, CN—6.0, LN—6.0)
Lengths:	■ 3.5 for Bias Binder; 4.0 for Quilt Stitch
Differential Feed:	■ Normal setting

- For curves, serge slowly and guide the fabric with your left hand as you hold the bias tape with your right. It may be necessary to serge a few stitches, stop, pivot, serge, stop, and pivot as you sew around the curve. Avoid very tight, small curves.

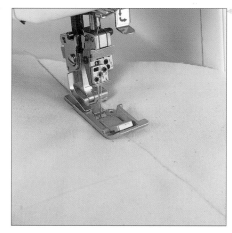

4 With washable marker, mark lines 1½" apart on fleece. Place fleece on top of outer fabric on machine. Adjust machine for Quilt Stitch using nylon filament thread in the needle and serge following marked lines. Using same stitch, make small 2" or 3" vertical accessory pockets on lining.

5 From coordinating fabric, cut two strips 1⅛" x 16" for ties. Select Cover Hem Wide and adjust machine accordingly. Place fabric in foot, right side up; pull through under foot and serge. Pin ties to quilted top piece, matching raw edges, 5" from top edge.

6 Layer quilted top and fused vinyl lining with pocket, wrong sides together. Cut 2" bias strips for edge finish. Press edges to center and insert into adjustable bias binder foot. Using chain stitch, attach binding to edge, serging carefully around all curves.

TRIMMED KNIT PJ'S

The serger and its accessories is the perfect tool for making children's clothing and night wear. The stitches are sturdy, standing up over time to any rambunctious child.

TIP

- When using the Lace Attachment guide, attach the lace and hem on flat pieces. Serge the seams after attaching lace.

- Lower the needles into the fabric and lace to avoid the lace from slipping when starting to serge.

1 Cut fabric according to pattern. Serge side seams on pants. Fold down top edge 1⅜", then back on itself again. Using Blindhem foot and blindhem stitch, serge top edge, making casing. Leave edge open approximately 2" for inserting elastic. Measure and insert elastic. Stitch elastic ends; serge casing closed.

2 Serge inseam on pajama bottoms. Fold up 1" hems on pant legs. With 1" hem guide, serge hems in place with Triple Cover Hem.

3 With embroidery thread, add decorative detail to flat scalloped-bordered edging. Gather raw edge with Gathering stitch and Gathering foot. Pull needle threads for fuller gathers.

4 On flat front and back sections, fold up ¼" hem along bottom. Insert folded edge into lace guide placing gathered

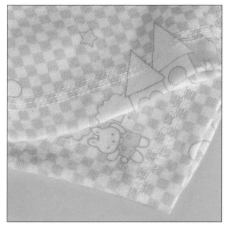

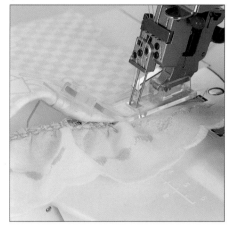

edging, right side up, under fabric as shown. Lower needles and serge with cover hem.

5 Stitch shoulder seams and insert sleeves flat with 4-thread stitch. Using 1" Hem guide and Triple Cover Hem, serge sleeve hems. Stitch sleeves and sides seams in one operation.

6 Measure contrasting ribbing or self-ribbing. Mark quarters and pin ribbing to neckline. Using the Triple Cover Hem, attach ribbing, serging from the right or wrong side depending on detail desired.

MATERIALS

- Child's or adult pajama pattern of choice
- Fabric yardage based on pattern
- Contrasting ribbing if desired
- ¾"- or 1"-wide elastic based on waist measurement
- Flat scalloped-bordered edging
- Rayon or cotton embroidery thread
- Polyester sewing thread

SERGER SET-UP

Stitch Selections:
- Cover Hem Wide; Cover Hem; Triple Cover Hem; Gathering stitch; Blindhem

Attachments:
- Cover Hem foot; Lace Attachment guide; Gathering foot; Blindhem foot

Thread:
- Polyester sewing thread

Tensions:
- Cover Hem Wide (CL—1.0, CN—6.0, LN—6.0); Cover Hem (CL—1.0, CN—6.0, LN—6.0); Triple Cover Hem (CL—1.0, CN—6.0, RN—6.0, LN—6.0), Gathering (UL—2.0, LL—2.0, RN—5.0, LN—6.0), Blindhem (UL—2.0, LL—2.0, LN—4.0)

Length:
- 4.0 for gathering

Differential Feed:
- 2.0 for gathering

VEST O' TECHNIQUES

Color-block or coordinate prints and techniques for an interesting textural effect on front and back. Tastefully utilize many of your serger techniques on one vest.

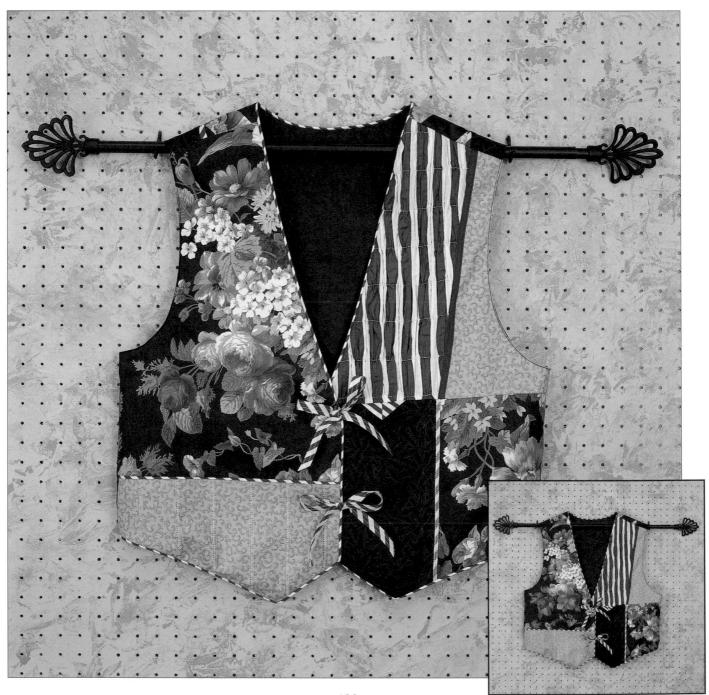

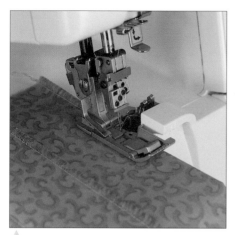  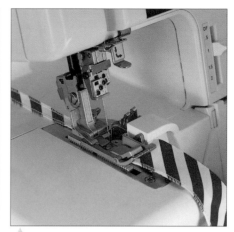

1 Cut fabric according to design plan. Mark fabric section on right side in 2" sections. Fold fabric, wrong sides together, at marks and position under foot slightly to left edge of needle plate. Flatlock along markings. Open, press flat.

2 On different section, use Tape Guide and contrasting bias strip to create trim. Attach trim with chain-stitch stitching on trim first, then onto fabric, right side up. Use this trim technique along edge of back panel also.

3 Create your own decorative tapes with bias strips and rolled hem. Trim and roll the edges to make ⅜"-wide tapes.

MATERIALS

- Vest pattern of choice; (e.g. Butterick or McCalls)
- 1 yard of four coordinating fabrics; 1½ yards of one for lining
- Coordinating spools of #40 rayon thread
- Round elastic thread

SERGER SET-UP

Stitch Selections:
- Flatlock 2; Rolled Hem 2; Chain Stitch; 5-thread ¼" (Elna ProCard A1)

Attachments:
- Tape Guide, Attachment Holder Base and Attachment Holder, Tape foot or Chain Stitch foot

Thread:
- LL—#40 rayon thread for Flatlock 2 and Rolled Hem 2; CL—round elastic thread for Chain Stitch

Tensions:
- Flatlock 2 (LL—5.0, LN—1.0); Rolled Hem 2 (LL—4.0, RN—4.0); Chain Stitch (CL—2.0, CN—4.0)

Lengths:
- 1.0 for Rolled Hem 2, 3.0 for Chain Stitch

Differential Feed:
- Normal setting

4 Attach trim, threading tape through hole in tape foot or chain-stitch foot. Center tape over seam and serge through center of tape with chain stitch.

5 Add a ruched section to vest front. Create fabric prior to cutting front section. Mark parallel lines on right side of fabric approximately 2" apart. Thread elastic into chain looper, increase stitch length, adjust differential feed to 2.0 and increase looper tension if necessary. From right side stitch along marked lines. Once fabric is completely ruched, cut fabric section.

6 Select ¼" stitch to create strip-quilted panel for back. Cut three 3½" x 8" print strips and four 3½" x 8 " solid strips.

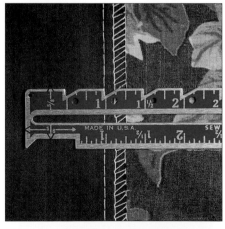

7 Alternate solid and print strips using 5-thread ¼" stitch. Press seams to side. Cut section according to pattern.

8 Construct vest according to pattern. Add contrasting piping to the outer edge if desired.

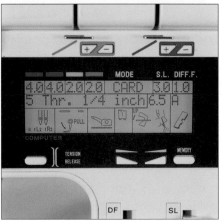

TIP

- For an easy lining technique, pipe the lower edges of the vest to the side seams front and back before stitching the side seams. Stitch the lining to the vest at neck, armholes, and bottom edges. Turn the vest to the right side through the side seams. Finish side seams.

UPHOLSTERY JACKET

Lighterweight upholstery fabrics can be used for unusual and
creative garments. Mix and match patterns for some interesting effects.

1 Cut body of jacket from fabric according to pattern. Cut sleeves, band, and bias trim from coordinating fabrics. Many upholstery fabrics are just as interesting on the wrong side as the right.

2 With right sides together, stitch shoulder seams. Press seams to side.

3 Trim one edge of seam allowance away. Fold remaining seam allowance over trimmed edge. Press and pin.

4 Using blindhem or edgestitching foot, place blade next to fold, move needle position left and stitch.

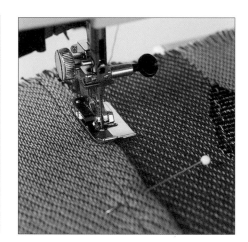

MATERIALS

- Simple jacket pattern of choice (e.g. Butterick 5178)
- Three coordinating fabrics yardage based on pattern
- Polyester sewing thread

SEWING MACHINE SET-UP

Stitch Selections:	▪ Straight stitch
Attachments:	▪ Blindhem or edgestitching foot
Threads:	▪ Polyester thread
Stitch Lengths:	▪ 2–2.5mm
Stitch Width:	▪ 0
Needle Position:	▪ Slightly to right or left for edgestitching
Feed Dogs:	▪ Raised

5 From the right side, place blindhem blade into seam and adjust needle position. Topstitch seams.

6 Stitch sleeve to front and back flat. Following steps 3 through 5 for flat–felled seam finish, stitch side seams and inner sleeve seams (if possible) in same manner.

TIP

- Adjust the needle position so the needle doesn't hit the blade of the blindhem foot while stitching.

- After making the bias trim with the bias tape maker, pin the bias strips to the garment easing around curves. Press to set the curve before stitching.

7 Press under ½" along inner edge of contrasting band. Pin in place. With blindhem or edgestitching foot, topstitch along folded edge.

8 Cut 2" bias trim to finish entire edge and sleeve edges. Pull fabric strip through bias tape maker and press folded edges into center.

9 Fold bias strip around edges. With blindhem or edgestitching foot, stitch bias trim in place. Press.

CLASSIC SPORT TOTE

TIP

- Carefully guide folded fabric edges through Felling guide "F–4". The lower fabric may be stitched flat to reduce any bulk in the seam.

- When serging a curve, stitch slowly keeping the curved edge next to the blade for an even edge. Stop serging periodically and adjust the fabric under the foot.

1 Cut one rectangle 32½" x 20¼" and one bottom piece from fabric using pattern pieces on page 123.

2 On one short end, press under ⅜" to wrong side. Repeat on opposite edge folding ⅜" to right side. Insert both fabric

edges into Felling guide and under serger foot. Lower needles and begin serging, guiding fabric evenly.

3 Cut 4" length of belting. Thread "D" ring through belting and fold in half. Attach bottom panel with balanced

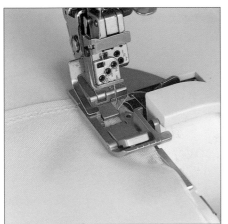

4 Cut one 1⅛" wide x 36" strip for drawstring tie. Using Cover Hem Wide and Beltloop foot, serge drawstring.

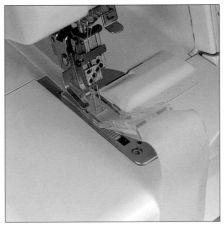

6 Fold down top edge to outside, ¼" and then again 1¼". Using Cover Hem Wide, serge close to edge encasing belting into

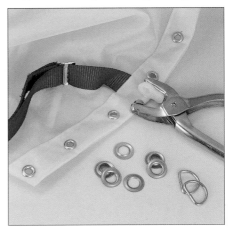

4–thread stitch, inserting raw edges of belting into seam at felled seamline. Guide curved edge slowly keeping stitches even.

5 Insert remaining belting through "D" ring. On one end of strap, make small loop through buckle and stitch end in place with sewing machine. Weave remaining end through buckle.

seam. Evenly space grommets around top of bag. Thread drawstring through grommets.

MATERIALS

- 1 yard of rainwear or outer wear fabric
- 1 yard webbing
- 1 each — "D" ring and buckle for strap
- Grommets and pliers
- Polyester sewing thread

SERGER SET-UP

Stitch Selections:
- Cover Hem Wide; Cover Hem

Attachments:
- Felling guide; Beltloop foot

Thread:
- Polyester sewing thread

Tensions:
- Cover Hem Wide (CL—1.0, CN—6.0, LN—6.0); Cover Hem (CL—1.0, CN—6.0, LN—6.0)

Lengths:
- Normal settings

Differential Feed:
- Normal setting

SILK EVENING BAGS

Choose an elegant silk fabric and add iridescent beads, a ruched strip,
or rows of woven ribbon floss to create a beautiful evening bag. The serger
techniques used here are easy to master in little time.

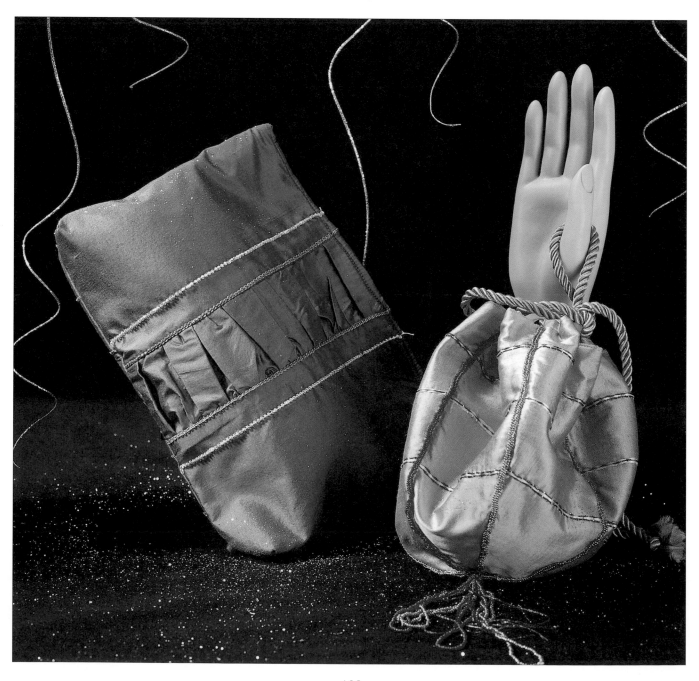

1 Interface fabric if necessary. For Vogue bag, cut pattern pieces according to pattern. Draw horizontal lines, 3" apart, beginning at top edge of each bag section. For Ghee's Portfolio pattern, add seam along bottom edge adding seam allowance to front and back pattern pieces. For front piece, cut strip, 3" by depth of bag for center ruched strip.

2 Fold fabric, right sides together, along mark. Flatlock along edge, open, and press flat. Using a bodkin or large-eyed tapestry needle, weave Glamour, ribbon floss, and Glamour, in that order, through ladder of flatlock stitch. Alternate weave sequence with Glamour and ribbon floss.

3 Using 3- or 4-thread stitch, seam bag sections together. Press seams to one side. Fold fabric along seam lines, wrong sides together. Place one or two strands of beads under beading foot along seamline. Using Pearl Flat 2, flatlock beads to all seamlines. Open out flat and adjust thread between beads. Continue constructing bag according to pattern instructions.

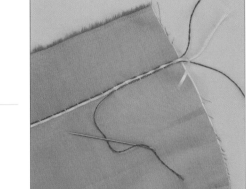

MATERIALS

- Bag pattern of choice (e.g. Vogue #8070, view F or Ghee's Portfolio Handbag #801—small)
- Fabric of choice—yardage based on pattern
- Lining based on pattern
- For closure —1¼ yards of ¼" decorative twisted cord or 10" straight hex-open frame for Ghee's bag
- Interfacing
- Assorted strands of cross-locked beads up to 3mm
- 1 spool of Ribbon Floss
- 1 spool each of Glamour, Decor or Deco 6
- Bodkin or large-eyed tapestry needle

SERGER SET-UP

Stitch Selections:	Flatlock 3; Pearl Flat 2 (Elna ProCard 5); Gathering (Elna ProCard 1); Chain Stitch
Attachments:	Piping foot and Tape Guide, Attachment Holder Base and Attachment Holder, Gathering Foot (optional)
Thread:	CL—Decor for Chain Stitch
Tensions:	Flatlock 3 (UL—2.0, LL—7.0, RN—1.0); Pearl Flat 2 (LL—4.0, RN—0.0); Gathering (UL—2.0, LL—2.0, RN—5.0, LN—6.0); Chain Stitch (CL—2.0, CN—4.0)
Lengths:	4.0 for Gathering; 3.0 for Chain Stitch
Differential Feed:	Normal setting

4 For portfolio bag, add ruching strip to center front. Using gathering stitch, gather both long edges of strip. Pull needle threads if necessary.

6 Mark vertical lines on wrong side of back section of portfolio bag, 3" apart. Thread Decor in chain-stitch looper. From wrong side, chain-stitch following markings. Chain-stitch seam allowance down on each side of ruched strip. Flatlock rows of beads if desired to front.

- It may be difficult to gather certain slippery fabrics as the threads seem to just "slide" through. In these situations, using a 4-thread stitch, secure the threads at one end of the strip. Pull the needle thread carefully to gather the fabric strip.

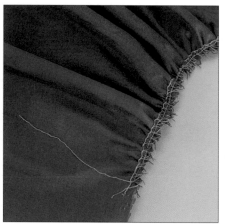

5 Center ruched strip on front of bag section. Cut front piece leaving seam allowances to accommodate center strip. Serge ruched section to side pieces. Check pattern piece against finished fabric front. Press seams to side.

7 Finish bag according to pattern instructions.

- When flatlocking beads or pearls, adjust the stitch length according to the size of the beads. Gently slide the threads between the beads.

STAMPED FAUX VEST

Accent a purchased blouse with serger techniques, creative fabric stamping, and a stitched-on vest front. Let your imagination run wild with ideas.

111

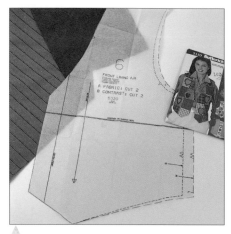

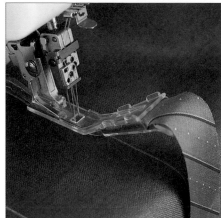

1 Use only front sections from vest pattern. Measure pattern against blouse to ensure fit. Cut one each from fashion fabric and lining. Cut 1⅛"-wide bias strips from lining fabric for decorative accent. Cut 1½"-wide bias strips from fashion fabric for armhole and center front binding.

2 Mark accent placement lines on vest fronts—two on left front, one on right. Using Cover Hem Wide and Beltloop foot, trim vest fronts with lining fabric accents following placement lines.

3 Apply fabric paint to stamps with sponge or brush. Following manufacturer's instructions, stamp vest fronts in pleasing manner.

MATERIALS

- 1 yard of fabric
- 1 yard of lining fabric
- Vest pattern of choice (e.g. Butterick #5330, Butterick #5231, or Rag Merchant Vest)
- Purchased blouse
- Rubber stamps — designs of choice
- Fabric paints
- Metallic variegated thread
- Decorative buttons

SERGER SET-UP

Stitch Selections:	Cover Hem Wide, Cover Hem
Attachments:	Beltloop foot, Cover Hem foot and Wrapped Edge guide
Thread:	CL—Metallic variegated thread
Tensions:	Cover Hem Wide (CL—1.0, CN—6.0, LN—6.0); Cover Hem (CL—1.0, CN—6.0, LN—6.0)
Length:	Normal setting
Differential Feed:	Normal setting

4 With wrong sides together, serge vest fronts to lining along bottom edges, at sides and at shoulders using ⅝" seamline. Turn and press.

5 Thread chain looper with metallic thread. Thread bias strip through Wrapped Edge guide. Working from wrong side so loops show on top, begin serging with Cover Hem Wide on bias strip first before inserting fabric and lining layer. Trim armhole openings.

6 Serge in the same manner binding center front edges on front pieces. Trim binding close to edges. Using a narrow, short zigzag or bartack stitch, close each binding end.

7 Stitch buttonholes and buttons. Straight-stitch sides and shoulders of vest fronts to blouse.

TIP

- Use the horizontal thread holder for unusually shaped spools. Test the cover hem tensions on a scrap of fabric first, then use the tension release clips if needed.

- Button vest fronts to both blouse sides and shoulder seams for different and unique design variation.

A JACKET OF TRICKS

Combine a number of subtle machine techniques on one jacket.
Create your own one-of-a-kind design with both fabrics and threads.

TIP

- Use machine techniques in moderation on your garments. It's better to be subtle than try to "show-off" everything you know!

- Try other techniques as fabric embellishment. Remember to create your fabric first before cutting the pattern section.

2 Before cutting pattern sections from the fabric, complete each technique. Some techniques may shrink fabric from original size so allow enough fabric before stitching the technique.

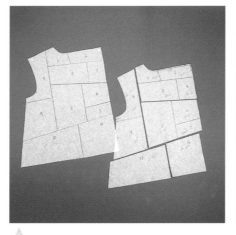

1 Trace pattern front and back onto pattern tracing paper. Mark off patchwork pattern and cut sections apart.

3 For back-and-forth tucks, mark and press 1½" folds across width of fabric.

MATERIALS

- Simple boxy jacket pattern of choice
- Six to seven coordinating fabrics—yardage based on pattern
- Three to four coordinating colors of Pearl Crown Rayon thread
- Rayon embroidery thread
- Polyester sewing thread
- Nylon filament thread
- 1 yard of cord
- 1 yard of fusible knit interfacing
- Pattern tracing paper

SEWING MACHINE SET-UP

Stitch Selections:	▪ Straight stitch; multi-zig zag; honeycomb stitch
Attachments:	▪ Blindhem or edgestitching foot; pearl or piping foot; 4mm beading foot; multi-cord foot
Threads:	▪ Polyester sewing thread on bobbin, decorative threads in needle or couched
Stitch Lengths:	▪ According to stitch
Stitch Width:	▪ According to stitch
Needle Position:	▪ According to stitch
Feed Dogs:	▪ Raised

4 With blindhem or edgestitching foot, move the needle position to the far left. With the blade of the foot close to the edge of each fold, stitch making tiny tucks.

6 Twist section of fabric into tight string. Wrap back on itself and hold with rubber band. Wet with water. Dry in dryer while still knotted.

5 Place marks on fabric at right angle to tucks 1½" apart. With straight stitch, alternate direction of tucks up and down while stitching. Cut pattern section from finished tucked fabric.

7 Once dry, open out crinkled fabric right side down. Place fusible knit on top and press crinkles in place.

8 Cut 1¾" bias strips from fabric of choice and two times the length of fabric–covered cord desired. Attach pearl and piping foot to machine and wrap one

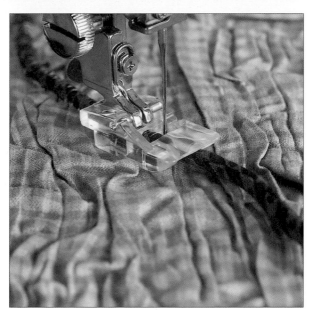

half the cord with bias strip right sides together. Stitch close to cord and across fabric and cord at center.

10 Using the beading foot and nylon filament thread, couch the fabric–covered cord with a zig zag stitch to the crinkled fabric. Cut pattern section from finished textured fabric.

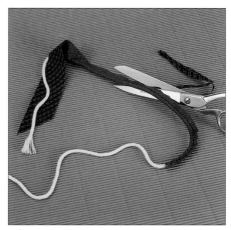

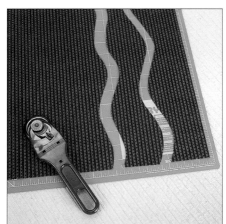

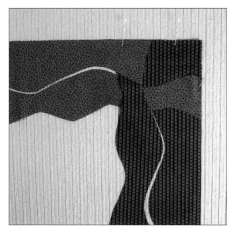

9 Trim the seam allowance close to stitching. With your fingers, begin turning the fabric back onto the cord making fabric–covered cording.

11 Using a rotary cutter and mat, cut curved strips from two fabric pieces — one in the vertical direction and one in the horizontal direction.

12 Beginning in one corner, pin one strip in horizontal direction. Pin second strip of different fabric in vertical direction. Continue weaving strips back and forth for patchwork design.

15 Add additional techniques if desired. Piece front and back sections together to form complete pattern piece. Continue constructing jacket according to pattern instructions.

16 Instead of buttons, use Chinese knots as closures. Make fabric–covered cording as in steps 8 and 9. Form two loops in the cord as shown here with the left loop on top of right. Weave tail of cording over and under loops as shown. Pull knot tight and hide ends in knot. Add a dab of glue to ends to hold. Slipstitch knots in place as buttons. Make loops from extra cording on other front section.

13 Fuse knit fuse to reverse side of weaving to hold strips in place. Using rayon embroidery thread, join strip "squares" with honeycomb stitch. Cut pattern section from woven fabric.

14 Attach multi-cord foot to machine. Thread three coordinating colors of Pearl Crown Rayon through foot. Couch threads with multi-zig zag stitch. Cut pattern section from embellished fabric.

MAKING BIAS STRIPS

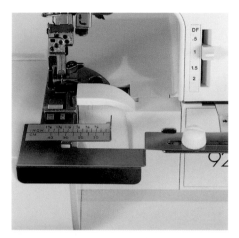

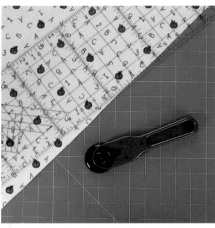

Use your serger to quickly cut bias strips for pipings or bias binding. Attach a ruled cloth guide to the machine using the attachment holder base. Determine the cut width of the strip by moving the attachment in line with the knife.

Cut your fabric along the true bias by folding across one corner at a 90 degree angle.

You can cut a continuous bias strip by matching the straight edges forming a tube. Offset the edges the width of one strip to begin.

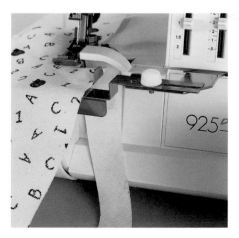

Place the fabric on the unthreaded serger and begin cutting your bias strips. It's up to you to guide straight but this method is quick and easy!

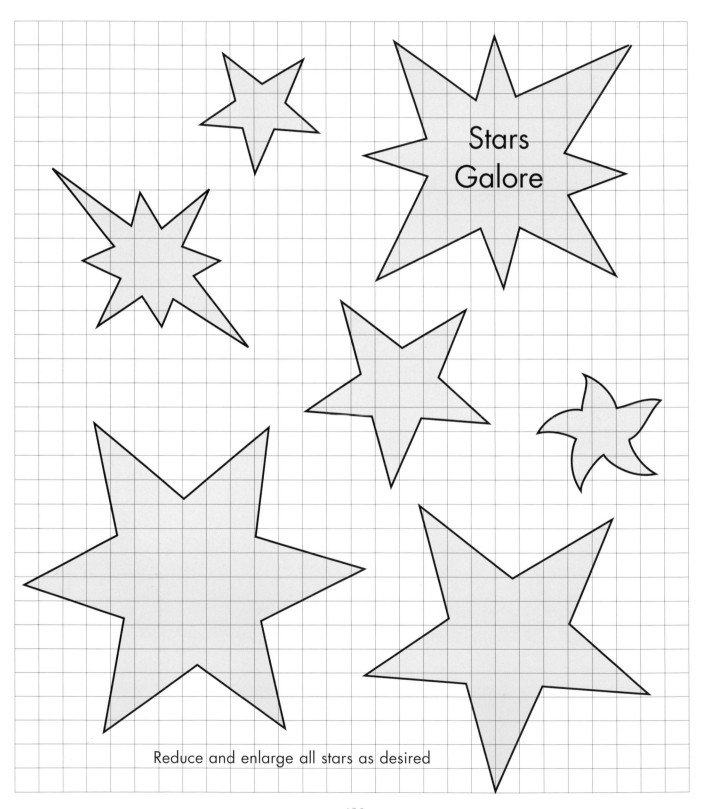

Stars
Galore

Reduce and enlarge all stars as desired

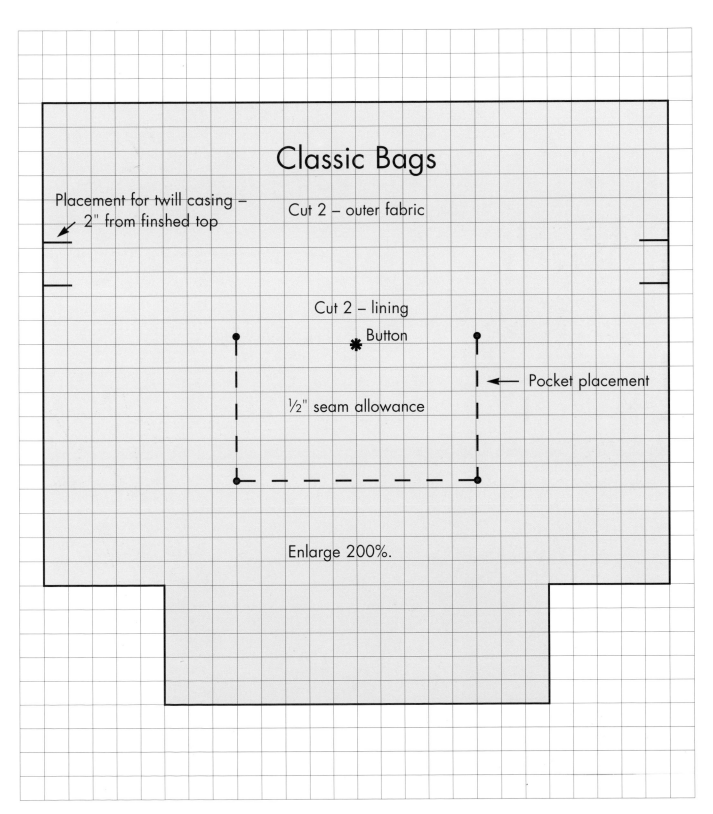

Classic Bags

Placement for twill casing – 2" from finshed top

Cut 2 – outer fabric

Cut 2 – lining

Button

Pocket placement

½" seam allowance

Enlarge 200%.

NECESSARY PATTERNS

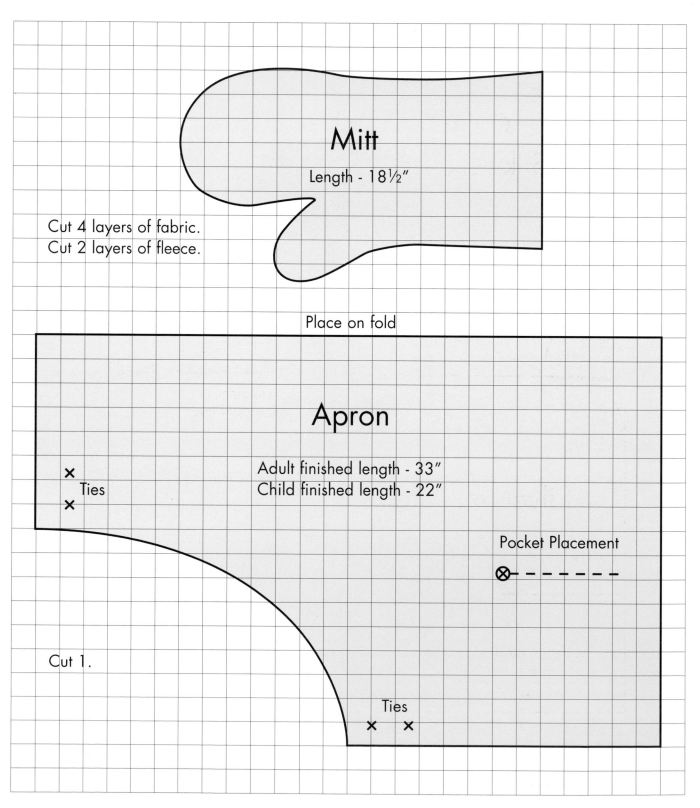

Mitt

Length - 18½"

Cut 4 layers of fabric.
Cut 2 layers of fleece.

Place on fold

Apron

Adult finished length - 33"
Child finished length - 22"

✕
Ties
✕

Pocket Placement
⊗ – – – – – –

Cut 1.

Ties
✕   ✕

NECESSARY PATTERNS

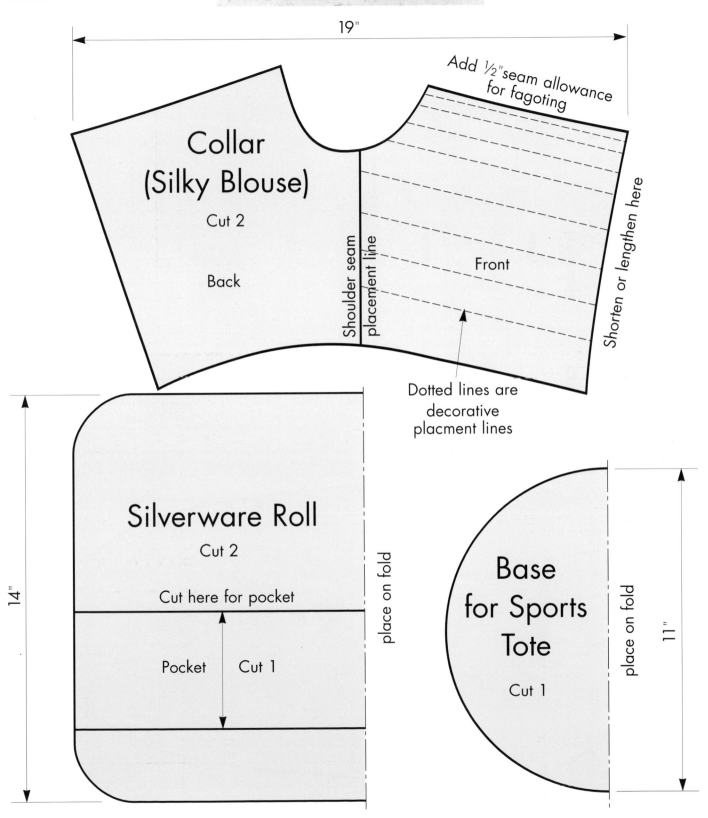

19"

Add ½"seam allowance for fagoting

Collar
(Silky Blouse)

Cut 2

Back

Shoulder seam placement line

Front

Shorten or lengthen here

Dotted lines are decorative placment lines

14"

Silverware Roll

Cut 2

Cut here for pocket

Pocket   Cut 1

place on fold

Base
for Sports
Tote

Cut 1

place on fold

11"

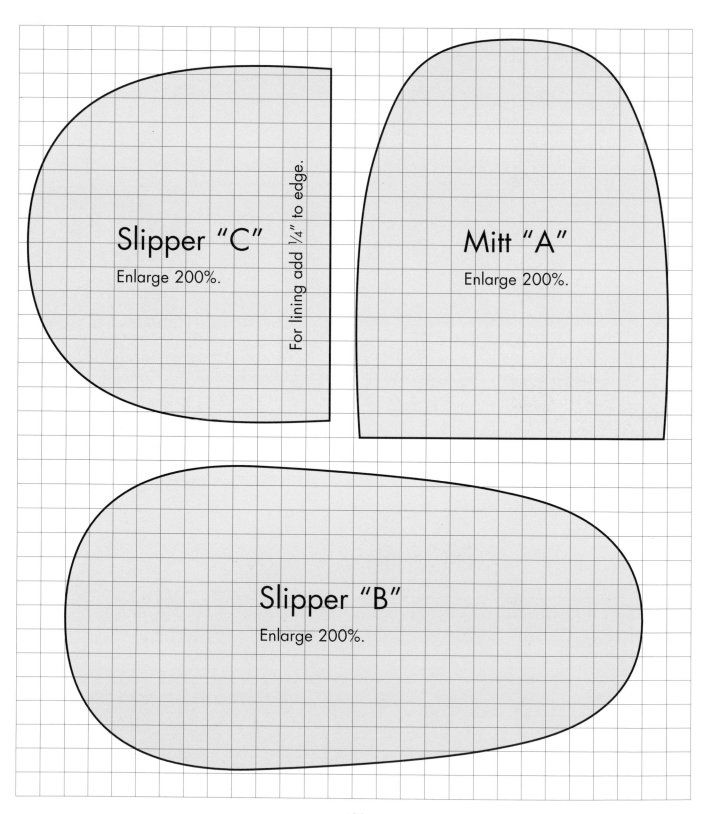

Slipper "C"

Enlarge 200%.

For lining add ¼" to edge.

Mitt "A"

Enlarge 200%.

Slipper "B"

Enlarge 200%.

METRIC EQUIVALENTS

Inches to Millimeters and Centimeters
MM - millimeters   CM - centimeters

Inches	MM	CM	Inches	CM	Inches	CM
⅛	3	0.3	9	22.9	30	76.2
¼	6	0.6	10	25.4	31	78.7
⅜	10	1.0	11	27.9	32	81.3
½	13	1.3	12	30.5	33	83.8
⅝	16	1.6	13	33.0	34	86.4
¾	19	1.9	14	35.6	35	88.9
⅞	22	2.2	15	38.1	36	91.4
1	25	2.5	16	40.6	37	94.0
1¼	32	3.2	17	43.2	38	96.5
1½	38	3.8	18	45.7	39	99.1
1¾	44	4.4	19	48.3	40	101.6
2	51	5.1	20	50.8	41	104.1
2½	64	6.4	21	53.3	42	106.7
3	76	7.6	22	55.9	43	109.2
3½	89	8.9	23	58.4	44	111.8
4	102	10.2	24	61.0	45	114.3
4½	114	11.4	25	63.5	46	116.8
5	127	12.7	26	66.0	47	119.4
6	152	15.2	27	68.6	48	121.9
7	178	17.8	28	71.1	49	124.5
8	203	20.3	29	73.7	50	127.0

METRIC CONVERSION CHART

Yards	Inches	Meters	Yards	Inches	Meters
⅛	4.5	0.11	1⅛	40.5	1.03
¼	9	0.23	1¼	45	1.14
⅜	13.5	0.34	1⅜	49.5	1.26
½	18	0.46	1½	54	1.37
⅝	22.5	0.57	1⅝	58.5	1.49
¾	27	0.69	1¾	63	1.60
⅞	31.5	0.80	1⅞	67.5	1.71
1	36	0.91	2	72	1.83

INDEX

A

Accent pillows, 50
Adjustable bias binder, 24
Appliqué foot, 16, 54
Appliquéd Dress, Easy, 68
Appliqués, serger, 68
Aprons, Reversible, 76
Attachment holder, 28, 49, 59, 61, 65, 101, 109

B

Bags, Classic, 70
Banner, 54
Bathroom, Pearly, 36
Bath Wrap, Mitt & Slippers, 92
Batting, 39, 40
Beading foot, 19, 115
Beads, 23, 108
Beltloop foot, 25, 33, 50, 51, 61, 96, 107, 112
Beltloop Pillows, 50
Bias binder attachment, 20, 23, 93
Bias binder foot, 69, 93, 96
Bias Strips, Making, 119
Bias-tape maker, 14
Blanket stitch, 11, 85, 86
Blanket-Stitch Vest, 84
Blindhem
    foot, 17, 23, 30, 45, 49, 56, 70, 71, 85, 91, 93, 94, 99, 104, 105, 115
    stitch, 36, 37, 45, 49, 56, 57, 85, 93, 99
Blouse, fagoted, 87
Blouse, Silky, 78
Bodkin, 14
Braids, 22
Buckwheat hulls, 39, 40
Buttonhole foot, 88
Button-sewing foot, 17, 37, 88, 89

C

Chair Cover, Simple, 32
Charts, Metric, 125
Chain stitch, 24, 28, 51, 52, 58, 59, 61, 65, 79, 93, 101, 109
Chain stitch foot, 85, 101, 102

Classic Bags, 70
Classic Sport Tote, 106
Classy Covers, 44
Collar, Silky, 78
Corded pintucks, 27
Cording guide, 79
Corners, matching, 18
Cotton, 13, 24
Couched threads, 11
Couching, 18, 19, 22, 23, 24
Cover hem
    foot, 25, 33, 51, 61, 62, 63, 68, 79, 80, 99, 112
    stitch, 12, 24, 25, 26, 27, 32, 33, 50, 51, 61, 68, 69, 79, 99, 107, 112
Covers, pillow, 50
Crosshatching, 52
Curve guide set, 28
Curtain, shower, 36

D

Darning foot, 18, 39, 47
Deco Braid, 34, 35
Deco-chain, 82, 83, 85
Deco-edge, 58, 63
Deco-overlock, 59, 61, 63, 82, 96
Decorating projects, 30-65
Decorator fabrics, 13
Differential feed, 22, 43
Dress-up projects (clothing, accessories), 66-118

E

Edgestitching, 17, 70, 72, 73
Edgestitching foot, 71, 72, 73, 104, 115
Edges, finishing, 20, 28
Elastic, 23
Elna needle system, 12
Elna stitches, 35, 37, 45, 49, 56, 59, 61, 65, 75, 77, 82, 85, 93, 96, 101, 109
Embroidery, 18, 38, 39, 40, 58, 59
Embroidery foot, 16, 39
Even-feed foot, 19
Evening Bags, Silk, 108

F

Fabrics, 13
Fagoted Shirt and Top, 87
Fagoting
    foot, 21, 79, 80, 88
    guide, 27
    stitch, 88
Faux Vest, Stamped, 111
Feed dogs, 19
Feet presser. *See* Presser Feet
Felling guide, 26, 107
Fine fabrics, 16
Flatlock stitch, 23, 35, 36, 37, 42, 43, 101, 109
Fleece, 13, 40, 41
Four-thread stitch, 51, 56, 68

G

Gathering foot, 18, 22, 35, 45, 49, 56, 99, 109
Gathering stitch, 35, 45, 56, 99, 109
Glamour thread, 35, 79, 81
Glue, fabric, 14
Hats and Roses, 82
Heirloom Hankie, 90
Hem gauge, 14
Hemming
    foot, 20, 54
    guide, 25, 32
Honey comb stitch, 115

J

Jacket of Tricks, 114
Jacket, Upholstery, 103

K

Kid's Organizer, 64
Knit PJ's, Trimmed, 98
Knits, 13, 17, 43

INDEX

L

Lace, 90, 91
    attachment guide, 25, 98, 99
    lacing guide, 26
Linen, 13, 39, 40, 41, 90, 91
Lint brush, 14
Loopers, 14, 28, 43, 47
    tension, 13
    thread in, 11
Looping sole foot, 19

M

Make-Up Roll, 95
Memory Boxes, Serger, 34
Metallic
    thread, 11, 47
    needles, 12
Microtec needles, 12, 77
Mitt, kitchen, 76
Mitt, Bath, 92
Monogram, 38, 39, 41
Multi-cord foot, 18, 115
Multi-purpose foot, 23, 45
Muslin, 39, 40

N

Napkins, 14, 58, 59, 60
Narrow three-thread stitch, 79
Neckroll, Elegant, 56
Needle
    plate, 21, 23, 75
    threaders, 14
Needles, 12, 13, 14, 17
Notions, 14
Nylon filament thread, 47

O

One-inch hem guide, 25, 51, 63, 79
Organizer, Kid's, 64
Overcasting foot, 17
Overlock foot, 17
Overlock stitch, 42, 56

P

Patchwork foot, 18, 88
Patterns, 120-124
Pearl Crown Rayon
    thread, 11, 12, 34, 63, 80, 82, 85, 96
Pearl-Edged Shawl, 74
Pearl flat 2 stitch, 74, 75, 109
Pearl foot, 19, 23, 74, 75, 115
Pearls, 23, 74
Pearly Bathroom, 36
Picnic Trimmings, Perfect, 60
Pillows, Sweet Dreams, 38
Pillows, Beltloop, 50
Pintuck foot, 27, 39, 79,
Pintuck guide, 79, 81
Pintucks, 20, 27, 81
Piping, 19, 24, 65, 109, 115
Piping foot, 19, 24
PJ's, Trimmed Knit, 98
Placemat, 60
Plaids, matching, 19
Plastic, 21
Point turner, 14
Polyester sewing thread, 11
Potpourri, 39, 40
Presser feet, 14, 15
    appliqué, 16, 54
    beading, 19, 115
    beltloop, 25, 33, 50, 51, 61, 96, 107, 112
    bias binder, 65, 93, 96
    blindhem, 17, 23, 30, 45, 49, 56, 70, 71,
        85, 91, 93, 94, 99, 104, 105, 115
    buttonhole, 88
    button-sewing, 17, 37, 88, 89
    chainstitch, 85, 101, 102
    cover hem, 25, 33, 51, 61, 62, 63, 68, 79,
        80, 99, 112
    darning, 18, 39, 47
    edgestitching, 71, 72, 73, 104, 115
    embroidery, 16, 39
    even-feed, 19
    fagoting, 21, 79, 80, 88
    gathering, 18, 22, 35, 45, 49, 56, 99, 109
    hemming, 20, 54
    looping sole, 19
    multi-cord, 18, 115
    multi-purpose, 23, 45
    overlock, 17
    patchwork, 18, 88
    pearl, 19, 23, 74, 75, 115
    pintuck, 27, 39, 79
    piping, 19, 24, 65, 109, 115
    quarter-inch, 18, 101
    ribbon and sequin, 20
    roller or Teflon™, 21
    satin stitch, 16, 18
    sequin and ribbon, 20
    serger, 22-29
    sewing machine, 16-21
    tape, 24, 27, 35, 59, 65, 101
    Teflon™ or roller, 21
    topstitch covered seam, 27, 68
    tricot, 21
    tucking, 20
    walking, 19
    zipper, 17
Purse, 70, 108

Q

Quarter-inch foot, 18, 101
Quilting, 18, 19, 28, 40, 46
    guide, 28, 45, 65
    needles, 12
    stitch, 45, 65, 96

R

Rainwear fabric, 54
Rayon Embroidery
    thread #40, 11, 39
Recycled Sweaters, 42
Reverse sewing, 11
Reversible Aprons, 76
Ribbon foot, sequin and, 20
Roller or Teflon™ foot, 21
Rolled hem, 13, 14, 22, 34, 35, 47, 59, 61, 77,
    85, 86, 90, 91, 101
Roll, Make-Up, 95
Rotary cutter & mat, 14
Ruching, 52, 56, 108
Ruffler, 19
Runner, Tasseled, 46

INDEX

S

Satin stitch foot, 16, 18
Scarves, 14
Seam ripper, 14
Seam sealant, 14
Serger
    appliqués, 68
    needles, 12, 13
    presser foot, 22-29
    thread, 11
Serger Memory Boxes, 34
Sequin and ribbon foot, 20
Sewing machine presser foot, 16-21
Shawl, Pearl-Edged, 74
Sheer fabric, 16
Silk fabric, 13, 16, 19, 78, 108
Silky Blouse and Collar, 78
Silk Evening Bags, 108
Silverware roll, 60
Simple Chair Cover, 32
Skirt, Fagoted, 87
Slippers, Bath, 92
Soutache, 24, 34, 35
Spray starch, 13
Sport Tote, Classic, 106
Stamped Faux Vest, 111
Stars Galore, 54
Stitches
    apply elastic, 45,
    bias binder, 96
    blanket, 11, 85, 86
    blind hem, 36, 37, 45, 49, 56, 57, 85, 93, 99
    chain, 24, 28, 51, 52, 58, 59, 61, 65, 79, 93, 101, 109
    cover hem, 12, 24, 25, 26, 27, 32, 33, 50, 51, 61, 68, 69, 79, 99, 107, 112
    cover hem wide, 25, 33, 51, 61, 68, 69 79, 96, 97, 99, 107, 112
    Deco-Braid K2, 34, 35
    Deco-Chain, 82, 83, 85
    Deco-Overlock, 59, 61, 63, 82, 96
    edgestitch, 17, 70, 72, 73
    Elna stitches, 35, 37, 45, 49, 56, 59, 61, 65, 75, 77, 82, 85, 93, 96, 101, 109
    embroidery, 18, 38, 39, 40, 58, 59
    fagoting, 88
    flatlock, 23, 35, 36, 37, 42, 43, 101, 109
    four-thread, 51, 56, 68
    gathering, 35, 45, 56, 99, 109
    honey comb, 115
    length, 13, 18
    monogram, 38, 39, 41
    narrow three-thread, 79
    overlck, 42, 56
    pearl flat 2, 74, 75, 109
    quilt, 45, 65, 96
    rolled hem, 13, 14, 22, 34, 35, 47, 59, 61, 77, 85, 86, 90, 91, 101
    straight, 16, 17, 47, 54, 71, 104, 115
    stretch wrapped, 76, 77
    topstitch, 17, 27, 28, 68, 82
    triple cover hem, 25, 51, 52, 99
    woolly rolled, 49, 82
    wrapped edge, 35, 77, 82
    zig zag, 16, 17, 19, 54, 55, 88, 115
Stool covers, 44
Straight stitch, 16, 17, 47, 54, 71, 104, 115
Straight stitch foot, 17, 18
Stretch needles, 12
Stretch wrapped stitch, 76, 77
Suede, 21
Sweaters, Recycled, 42
Sweet Dreams Pillows, 38

T

Tablecloths, 48, 58
Tape
    and cord guide, 24, 35
    basting, 14
    foot, 24, 27, 35, 59, 65, 101
    guide, 24, 27, 59, 101, 109
    paper or masking, 14
Tassels, 47, 48, 52, 74
Tasseled Runner, 46
Teflon™ foot, roller or, 21
Tension, 11, 12, 13, 18, 29, 41, 46, 57
Tension release guides, 29
Thread guides, 29
Thread, 11, 18, 29, 47, 82
Tiered Tablecloth, 48

Topstitch covered seam foot, 27, 68
Topstitching, 17, 27, 28, 68, 82
Topstitching needles, 12
Top, Fagoted, 87
Tote, Sport, 106
Tricot foot, 21
Trimmed Knit PJs, 98
Trimmings, Perfect Picnic, 60
Trims, 22, 24
Triple Cover Hem, 25, 51, 52, 99
Tucking foot, 20
Two-thread converter, 28, 37, 45, 49, 75, 77, 82
Tweezers, 14

U

Ulstrasuede™. 42
Upholstery fabric, 13
Upholstery Jacket, 103

V

Valance, Trimmed Cherry, 58
Valance, window, 36, 58
Vest, Blanket-Stitch, 84
Vest O' Techniques, 100
Vest, Stamped Faux, 111
Vinyl, 21

W

Walking foot, 19
Windsock, 54
Wooly Nylon™ threads,11, 35, 49, 75, 76, 77, 83, 85
Woolly rolled, 49, 82
Wrap, Bath, 92
Wrapped edge guide, 112
Wrapped edge stitch, 35, 77, 82
Wrapped seam guide, 26, 61, 62, 68, 69

Z

Zig zag stitching, 16, 17, 19, 54, 55, 88, 115,
Zipper foot, 17